A
MARITIMER'S
MISCELLANY

Fascinating Facts About
Nova Scotia,
New Brunswick &
Prince Edward Island

Clary Croft

NIMBUS
PUBLISHING

Nimbus Publishing Limited

PO Box 9166, Halifax, NS B3K 5M8

(902) 455-4286 www.nimbus.ns.ca

Printed and bound in Canada

Design: Reuben Hall

Cover and interior illustrations: Richard Rudnicki

Author photo: Sharon Croft

Library and Archives Canada Cataloguing in Publication

Croft, Clary
A Maritimer's miscellany : fascinating facts about Nova Scotia,
New Brunswick, and Prince Edward Island / Clary Croft.
Includes bibliographical references. ISBN 978-1-55109-632-2
1. Maritime Provinces—History—Miscellanea. 2. Maritime Provinces—
Miscellanea. I. Title.
FC2028.C78 2007   971.5   C2007-904339-9

Canadä The Canada Council | Le Conseil des Arts
for the Arts | du Canada NOVA SCOTIA
Tourism, Culture and Heritage

We acknowledge the financial support of the Government of Canada through the Book Publishing Industry Development Program (BPIDP) and the Canada Council, and of the Province of Nova Scotia through the Department of Tourism, Culture and Heritage for our publishing activities.

⌐ TABLE OF CONTENTS ⌐

"SHORT IS GOOD" is a golden rule in mass communications. Perhaps it's more important in radio than in print because time is more precious than paper. But isn't it strange that so many writers believe the dictionary was meant to be unloaded on their readers by the tonne. Clary Croft, on the other hand, is a master word-crafter who subscribes completely to the "short is good" maxim, creating fact-filled images with language that defies editing.

At the same time, he's passionate about his subjects. That explains why we've been working together on radio for more than four years, recording his charming little vignettes (each no more than thirty or forty seconds long) about the fascinating adventures and misadventures of Maritimers through the ages. After Clary reads each one into the microphone, I hear myself saying "really?" or I just quietly smile. I hope you do the same, because with Clary Croft, short is very good indeed.

Jack McGaw, owner and operator of
Information Radio Stations in Maritime Canada
Halifax, Nova Scotia

❧ ACKNOWLEDGEMENTS ❧

I'D LIKE TO THANK the folks at the Information Radio Stations, especially Jack McGaw. To my publisher, Nimbus—many thanks for your continued support and interest. It is always a pleasure to work with you. My sincere gratitude goes to the staffs of the libraries, museums, and archives where I have spent years poring over material—and continue to do so. I'd also like to acknowledge the many writers and researchers from whom I have gleaned information. Every tiny bit adds to this rich mosaic we call the Maritimes. And as always—and most importantly—I offer thanks, love, and admiration to my wife, Sharon, who shares my passion and my life.

Finally, this book is dedicated to the memory of three remarkable women who have enriched my life beyond measure.

To Mary Martha Creighton, a dear friend who, although not born a Maritimer, embraced us with a zest and eagerness to explore and learn more about her adopted part of Canada.

To Marjorie Campagna, the best mother-in-law a man could ever have, and a great companion on our many journeys throughout the Maritimes.

To Olive Croft, my mother, who taught me at an early age that we live in one of the most beautiful and interesting places in the world. My mom kept scrapbooks made from old catalogues or binders of foolscap held together with yarn. Into these, she'd paste clippings about people, places, and things—especially about the Maritimes. She inspired me to learn and explore—a gift for which I am eternally grateful.

⮞ INTRODUCTION ⮜

I NEVER CEASE TO BE FASCINATED with the history and culture of the Maritimes. Fortunately, for over five decades, I have had the opportunity to work and travel throughout Nova Scotia, New Brunswick, and Prince Edward Island. Even more fortunate is that for three and a half of those decades, I have made those journeys with my wife, Sharon. We love exploring our region, learning new things and meeting new people. We have travelled the world, and truly believe we live in one of the loveliest places on earth.

This book is an extension of a previous book called *Nova Scotia Moments*. That book contained a collection of some of the short radio spots, called Nova Scotia Moments, that I did for the Halifax Information Radio Station. Information Radio Stations have now spread throughout the Maritimes, and besides Halifax and Amherst in Nova Scotia, we are heard daily on our New Brunswick stations in Moncton, Fredericton, and St. Stephen, and on the Confederation Bridge linking New Brunswick and Prince Edward Island. Each day has a new Maritime moment.

CHAPTER ONE

SHAPED BY THE WIND AND WAVES

✧ Maritime marriage ✧

Even before Confederation, the three provinces situated along the northeast Atlantic coast of North America were referred to as the Maritimes. When Maritime politicians planned a conference on the possibility of Maritime union in Charlottetown in 1864, officials from Upper Canada took notice and invited themselves to the table. The result, three years later in 1867, was the creation of the Dominion of Canada. Mind you, the fledgling nation then only included the two regions designated Upper and Lower Canada (Ontario and Quebec) by the 1791 British Constitutional Act, and the former colony of Nova Scotia which, in 1776, was divided into the two provinces of New Brunswick and Nova Scotia. It would take another six years to convince Prince Edward Island to join the Dominion in 1873.

What's the difference ✧ between the Maritimes and the ✧ Atlantic Provinces?

The term Atlantic Provinces didn't come into widespread use until Newfoundland and Labrador joined Confederation in 1949. Newfoundland's first premier, Joseph Smallwood, is said to have originated the phrase.

✧ Melting into the Maritimes ✧

This was all a moot point some 16,000 years ago when our present-day Maritimes were covered by the Wisconsin ice sheet. Geologists estimate that the area around the Bay of Fundy became ice free 14,500 years ago; Halifax's Bedford Basin was a lake some 9,000 years ago; and Prince Edward Island wasn't an island until a mere 7,000 years ago.

❖ The erratic boulders of Peggy's Cove ❖

Each year, thousands of tourists drive to the scenic town of Peggy's Cove, one of the world's most photographed locations. The quaint fishing village reminds people of a bygone time, and the rugged coastline is a constant reminder of the power and majesty of the sea. But there is another geographic wonder that intrigues everyone who visits this Nova Scotia village. Surrounding the area for many kilometres are strange, isolated rock formations perched on granite ledges—seemingly defying gravity in many cases. These oddly placed boulders, which give the land the appearance of a moonscape, were left there by melting glaciers and have an appropriately strange name—erratics.

❖ Lofty locales ❖

Although there are some relatively high geographic locations in New Brunswick and on Nova Scotia's Cape Breton Island, the Maritime provinces aren't known as mountain country. What lofty locales we do have are part of the ancient Appalachian range. But these peaks don't soar like the Rockies of Canada's west coast. As you might expect, Prince Edward Island comes in with the smallest mountain (well, a hill really) at 142 metres. Cape Breton Highlands National Park boasts Nova Scotia's highest elevation, where White Hill reaches to 532 metres. New Brunswick's Mount Carleton caps the list. It stretches to the top elevation in the Maritime provinces at 820 metres.

❖ Tidal tales ❖

The tides in Maritime Canada are world-famous for their force and size. The Bay of Fundy's tides are considered the highest in the world.

Tides have also played an important part in several Maritime folk beliefs. One Mi'kmaq belief says the tides are the result of a giant whale splashing its tail.

Eminent Scottish geologist, Sir Charles Lyell, travelled to Nova Scotia in 1841, and had this to say about the famous Fundy tides: "The tides are said to be the highest in the world. They often come up at first with a lofty wave called the Bore, of which I saw a fine example in the largest river of Nova Scotia, the Shubenacadie, where the waters seems to be running down a much steeper slope than the St. Lawrence at its rapids." Not everyone agreed with Lyell! In the next century, after a visit to Moncton's Bore Park on the Petitcodiac River, celebrated American humorist Erma Bombeck commented on how "a trickle of brown water, barely visible, slowly edged its way up the river toward us with all the excitement of a stopped-up toilet."

⇥ Cape Breton's arm of gold ⇤

The arm of gold—or Bras d'Or—is the name given to the large lake in the centre of Cape Breton Island. It has been celebrated in verse and song, and is a popular recreation spot with an international reputation for outstanding vistas. This stunningly beautiful body of water covers a full tenth of the Island's territory, and has enough saline content to be acknowledged as the largest saltwater lake in North America.

⇥ The world's largest hayfield ⇤

The Tantramar Marshes that join New Brunswick and Nova Scotia have been called "the world's largest hayfield." Acadian farmers dyked and farmed the region in the early 1700s, collecting vast quantities of hay. After the Acadian deportation in 1755, Yorkshire settlers moved in and harvested the rich hayfields. By the beginning of the nineteenth century, 90 percent of the marshes were dyked. The hay was harvested for domestic use, to supply lumber camps, and for the Newfoundland and New England markets.

⟶ A pretty place named for an ugly noise ⟵

The Tantramar Marshes are home to many different species of waterfowl. Because of the noise made by thousands of beating wings, the early Acadian settlers called the region *tintamarre*, which loosely translates as "big ugly noise." Although we know the region as the Tantramar Marshes, the Acadian name lives on at the Tintamarre Festival in Caraquet when partygoers make their own big ugly noise while celebrating National Acadian Day on August 15.

⟶ Nova Scotia: a gypsum giant ⟵

Nova Scotia's gypsum deposits are among the largest workable deposits in Canada. The first mining of gypsum in North America began in Nova Scotia about 1770. Since that time, Nova Scotia has become the most productive gypsum-mining region in the world. In the mid-1900s production increased dramatically with the invention of wallboard, more commonly known as Gyproc or drywall. The gypsum industry in the province continued to grow rapidly and first reached almost one million metric tonnes production per year in 1939. Now half a dozen companies work the mines in Nova Scotia—the largest is National Gypsum (Canada) Limited located at East Milford.

⟶ Blueberries worth their weight in gold ⟵

Nova Scotia is home to several successful gold discoveries. One of the biggest was made in a blueberry barrens just outside Sherbrooke in 1861, when Nelson Nickerson and his family found gold while picking blueberries. They hid the fact for some time, bringing the ore back home in pails under a covering of berries; however, suspicious neighbours watched them and discovered their secret. By October 18, 1861, the news was out, and more than two hundred people assembled to stake claims. At one time it was one of the most productive mining areas in the world. The mines closed in 1941. The community that grew around it was appropriately named Goldenville.

✦ Halifax's own North Pole ✦

The Halifax Regional Municipality is the largest municipal region in the Maritimes. At 5,577 square kilometres, it is slightly smaller than Prince Edward Island at 5,660 square kilometres. Because of amalgamation in 1996, the area encompasses Halifax and Dartmouth, Bedford and Sackville, and basically the entire county of Halifax. This vast territory would seem odd to early inhabitants who knew Halifax as a far smaller place. In fact, anthropologist Paul Erickson, in his book *Historic North End Halifax*, tells us that in the 1820s, one house at the corner of Gottingen and Gerrish streets was considered so far removed from the centre of town that it was nicknamed the North Pole.

✦ Sunny Saint John ✦

Waiting for more sunshine in your forecast? Maybe we should all be in New Brunswick, where in an average year, sunless days number 75 and sunny days number between 140 and 160. Chatham records an above average two thousand sunny hours per year. Saint John records the fewest sunny hours for July; however, it makes up for this by reporting an average of nearly one hundred hours of sunshine in December—more than any other spot in eastern Canada.

✦ Dreaming of a white Christmas ✦

If you live in the largest city in the Maritimes, you may have to keep dreaming. Environment Canada says that Haligonians have only a 50 percent chance of enjoying a white Christmas.

✦ Winds wild enough to blow your house down! ✦

They blast out of the southeast, sometimes reaching hurricane strength. In areas around Cheticamp in Cape Breton, they are the reason some people have ropes that can go over their houses to hold them down firmly to the ground. They are called *les suêtes*—strong winds born off the coast of Cape Breton. A derivation of the Acadian phrase *sud est* (southeast), *les suêtes* are unique enough to the region that Environment Canada issues specific and separate warnings for Inverness County–Mabou and North. In March of 1996, *les suêtes* were measured at 245 kilometres an hour.

⤳ Sweet spring in Sherbrooke ⤲

In 1850, fifteen-year-old Sophia Cunningham of Sherbrooke wrote these lines about spring in Nova Scotia:

> How pleasant in the time of spring to leave a cheerful home,
> And for a quiet meditation into the woods to roam.
> The gentle zephyrs stir the leaves,
> The birds they sweetly sing,
> And we can almost seem to hear the very voice of spring.

I was born in Sherbrooke, and I can tell you for a fact that spring in that town is delightful. It's nice to know some things remain constant.

⤳ A year with no summer ⤲

In 1816, the Maritimes and other parts of the northern hemisphere experienced "the year of no summer." Spring snows fell with a brown tinge; red sunrises and spectacular sunsets were the norm; and crops failed from lack of sun. What most residents didn't know at the time was that late in 1815, Tambora volcano in the East Indies erupted and sent a dust cloud into the atmosphere that had a catastrophic effect as far away as North America's east coast.

⤳ Weary of winter in New Brunswick ⤲

French explorer Nicholas Denys established a post at St. Peters, now known as Bathurst, New Brunswick, in 1652 and retired there in 1668. But he wasn't a fan of the local winters. He wrote: "My house is flanked by four little bastions with a palisade with six pieces of cannon in batteries. The lands are not of the best: there are rocks in some places. I have a large garden in which the land is good for vegetables, which come on in a marvellous way. I have sown the seeds of Pears and Apples, which have come up and are well established, although this is the coldest place that I have lived, and the one where there is the most snow."

✵ Trekking to school with frozen toes ✵

Many of us grew up hearing our grandparents joke about having to slog through heavy snow just to get to school. They'd say it was uphill both ways, and that they often made the journey in bare feet. Well, a young Loyalist immigrant to New Brunswick named Hannah Ingraham could best them all. In a remembrance of her life in the winter of 1786, she told of hauling her brother to school on a hand sled. Hannah's brother had chopped off his toe while cutting wood, and her father promised that if she hauled her injured brother to classes every day, she could attend an additional term at school. She wrote: "But, oh, it was hard work through the deep snow and once it was so heavy that the poor boy got his [other] toe froze before we reached the school." No sick days for these hardy scholars!

The first school in Aylesford, Nova Scotia, opened in 1791 and was affiliated with the Anglican Church. Attendance often depended upon weather and the living conditions of the children. On March 30, 1792, the Reverend Wiswall wrote of his parish: "Aylesford is an exceedingly poor settlement, and for want of shoes, very few children can attend the school in winter months."

✵ Warden of the North ✵

If you're a fan of writer Rudyard Kipling, you may be interested to know he wrote about Halifax in the 1890s in his poem "The Song of the Cities."

Into the mist my guardian prows put forth,
Behind the mist my virgin ramparts lie,
The Warden of the Honour of the North,
Sleepless and veiled am I!

Those lines inspired Nova Scotian author Thomas Raddall to call his epic history of our city *Halifax: Warden of the North.*

➢ Shores for shipwrecks ✦

Because of the huge number of vessels wrecked on its shores, Sable Island is well-known as the Graveyard of the Atlantic. However, a much smaller island holds a similar claim—not that it's anything to boast about. The northernmost location in Nova Scotia is a small island approximately twenty-one kilometres northwest of Cape North, Cape Breton. Positioned in the Cabot Strait, in the Gulf of St. Lawrence, St. Paul Island is barely one and a half by five kilometres in size. Because of the numerous shipwrecks that have taken place on or near its tiny coastline, the Island has the unfortunate moniker of Graveyard of the Gulf.

Isle Haute is a tiny island in the Bay of Fundy. It rises steeply over ninety-one metres from sea level, and is known as a dangerous spot for local navigation. In fact, because so many early vessels were wrecked near its high cliffs, the early Acadians had another name for it—*Isle aux Morts*, or Island of the Dead.

➢ Miminegash and other tongue-twisting towns ✦

I love hearing visitors to our region try to pronounce some of our place names. How many variants are there for Antigonish? But we shouldn't be smug. To be fair, unless you heard the words being said, how could you possibly know how to pronounce Miramichi, Miminegash, or Chezzetcook? I bet we come across as being just as quaint when we travel. However, even linguists are unable to explain why residents of our largest city are called Haligonians. City historian Lou Collins says that the origin is unknown and that residents of Halifax, England, are generally known as Halifaxians. So, when you hear someone struggling with a Maritime place name, just smile—because we don't have all the answers either!

⤙ Dunksville and other Maritime capitals ⤚

Halifax was actually lucky to be called Halifax—it could have been worse. The city was named for Charles Montague, the man in charge of British colonial settlements at the time of the town's founding. Charles was married in 1741 to Miss Anne Dunk, a rich heiress. Following the custom of the day, he assumed her family name in addition to his own. Luckily for us, they didn't use his wife's family name, or we might be living in Dunktown, Dunksville, or Dunksborough. Fortunately, Charles Montague Dunk was also the Earl of Halifax—so we got the far classier name!

Charlottetown was originally called Charlotte Town in honour of Queen Charlotte, wife of George III. He was the reigning monarch when the town was designated as the capital of the colony of St. John's Island in 1765.

As the premier Loyalist town and commercial hub of the fledgling province of New Brunswick, it certainly seemed that Saint John would be chosen to serve as its capital. However, Governor Thomas Carleton thought otherwise. He wanted a more central location and one further away from the coast that could be more easily protected. So he chose the upriver community of Maugerville, an old French settlement situated on a beautiful section of the St. John River. Governor Carleton named the new capital after Frederick, the second son of the reigning monarch George III. At first it was known by its two-word title, Frederick Town, but soon became known simply as Fredericton.

⇢ Egypt and Russia, right next door ⇠

Sometimes you don't even have to leave your own province to travel to exotic locations. Here are some examples from my home province of Nova Scotia. Vesuvius, in Kings County, is obviously named for the great volcano that erupted near Naples, Italy. You can also visit Russia in Kings County. How about a trip to Egypt? This town, once the dual communities of Northeast Egypt and Southwest Egypt, is found in Cape Breton Highland's National Park. It was named after Joseph Hart, whose journey to these lands was compared to another more famous Joseph's journey into Egypt. Quite the legend to live up to, don't you think?

⇢ An unfortunate name ⇠

Nova Scotia certainly has its share of interesting place names. Take the rather unpleasant-sounding name of the locale known as Malignant Cove. Located near Cape George in Antigonish County, the pretty little community was named after an American Revolutionary War vessel, *Malignant*, that ran ashore in the cove. In 1915, in an effort to give the place a more welcoming name, it was rechristened Melburn. But the locals kept the old name of Malignant Cove, and that is what it's still called today.

⇢ The Garden of the Gulf ⇠

The Mi'kmaq knew the island as Abegweit, and early French visitors knew it as Isle St. Jean. It seems that the island's European discoverer, Jacques Cartier, didn't give it a name, even though he thought it a lovely place. When Cartier sighted island soil in 1534, he lauded its beauty, saying it was "the fairest land it is possible to see...full of fine meadows and trees." After the Treaty of Paris in 1764, the British changed the name to St. John's Island. And, during the 1780s, there were movements afoot to change the name to New Ireland, New Guernsey, or even New Anglesea. But, by 1798, maps were showing the name Prince Edward Island, and a year later, the name became official.

✦ The tale of Mouse Harbour ✦

Souris, Prince Edward Island, is a pretty community with a rather peculiar name. In French, *la souris* is mouse. Early Acadian settlers had to contend with numerous plagues of mice that infested the area. Hordes of the rodents would devour crops, then make their way to the sea where they drowned. One French vessel in the early 1700s reported having to sail through a sea covered with mouse carcasses. A French map of 1744 names the area Havre à la Souris. The English translated that and called the area Mouse Harbour, but later changed the name to Colville Bay. That didn't stick, but Souris did, and Souris it remains.

✦ A revolutionary province ✦

It may well be argued that the province of New Brunswick owes its existence to the American Revolution. During and after the American War of Independence, many United Empire Loyalists (colonial citizens loyal to Britain) moved up to the area of the British colony of Nova Scotia that lay in the lands surrounding the St. John River. Many were wealthy gentry who wanted to be rewarded for their loyalty and to have a stronger say in their own destiny. These men petitioned Britain for the right to form a new colonial province that they boasted would be "a stable agricultural society led by landed gentry." As a result, a section of the former colony of Nova Scotia was renamed New Brunswick in 1784. One proposal for the name of the fledgling colony of New Brunswick was New Ireland, but in the end, it was decided to name it after the German House of Brunswick. At that time, Britain's royal family was tied dynastically with this German state.

✦ German names in an English town ✦

In 1764, most of the remaining German settlers in Halifax who didn't move to Lunenburg petitioned the governor to have the area north of the present location of Scotia Square named Gottingen, as a show of affection for that district in Germany. The petition was granted, and today Gottingen Street retains the name.

Anti-German sentiment after World War Two caused some interesting name changes in Halifax. Before the war, in an area south of Spring Garden Road once settled by early German immigrants and known as Schmidtville, one could find Rottenburg Street. However, postwar sentiment had its sway, and in 1947, the street was renamed Clyde Street.

✺ Mauger's double legacy ✦

Stretching out into the entrance of Halifax Harbour, on McNab's Island, is Mauger's Beach. New Brunswick boasts a town called Maugerville. Both were named in honour of Joshua Mauger, who arrived at Halifax from the Isle of Jersey in 1749. An astute businessman, Joshua's dealings included rum sales, shipping, and privateering. After making his fortune, he retired to England and stood for Parliament.

✺ Directions for locals only ✦

With the click of a mouse and some online searching, you can find almost any address you are looking for. Satellite systems can hone in on a dwelling in seconds. But years ago, you had to know your history and local geography to find some addresses. For example, in a June 18, 1810, announcement in the *Nova Scotia Royal Gazette*, the cabinetmaking firm of Tulles, Pallister, and McDonald announced they still carried on business on Barrington Street, one door south of Sackville. Later that year, in October, it was announced that one of the partners, John Tulles, had removed to the house "lately occupied by Mrs. Gracie, and nearly opposite the Ordnance Gate." What happened if you were new to town and didn't know where Mrs. Gracie lived? You asked around, I guess!

✺ The Black Hole of Nova Scotia ✦

Temperance leaders had a way of giving a community that sold and used liquor some pretty nasty names. Halifax was known as Black Town, and in 1885 the community of Parrsboro, on the Bay of Fundy, was also given an interesting moniker by the *Chignecto Post and Borderer*. Because of the number of whisky shops in Parrsboro, the paper labelled it the Black Hole of Nova Scotia.

✣ Where do ewe sleep? ✣

Thousands of men and women used to find employment at the numerous lobster factories that dotted the coastlines of the Maritimes. These small operations provided one of the few employment opportunities for women, and many a Maritime love match was made at the lobster factory. My wife's grandparents, in fact, met at a factory on Pictou Island. Women were often provided with room and board, or found housing in local homes. Men often slept in open dormitories filled with bunk beds. Housing dozens of men, these sleeping quarters were called ram pastures.

✣ Miramichi mouthful ✣

Like the Halifax Regional Municipality and the Cape Breton Regional Municipality, the City of Miramichi is the result of the amalgamation of several communities. In 1995, the towns of Chatham and Newcastle, and the villages of Douglastown, Loggieville, and Nelson-Miramichi were blended and named Miramichi. But here's the rub. History has come full circle. In the 1780s, the area's first sheriff, Benjamin Marston, could have saved them all that confusion if everyone had listened when he declared, "Miramichi is too hard to spell; let's call it Newcastle."

✣ The passenger pigeon is grounded for good ✣

The passenger pigeon is an enduring symbol of our human ability to cause the extinction of a once-common bird. Former Nova Scotia provincial museum director, Harry Piers, has written: "James P. Kelly...told me...that when he was a boy, say about fifteen years ago [around 1857] about the end of August, he and Tom J. Egan, on returning from shooting across the North West Arm, Halifax, saw a bird…on [the] east side of the Arm. Kelly shot it and it proved to be a Passenger Pigeon…It was the only Passenger Pigeon Kelly ever saw, although his father had told him that they used to be common about Halifax."

✣ A walk in the old-growth woods ✣

With all the lumbering that was carried on in the Maritimes, there are few areas of original-growth forest left. But one area in Cape Breton boasts original hardwood forest on a hilltop known as the MacFarlane Woods. This original-growth forest is now a protected nature reserve designated under the Special Places Protection Act. The MacFarlane Woods provide an opportunity to visit a first-growth Maritime forest.

✣ A wilderness haven ✣

On October 31, 1927, Nova Scotia established what is now the largest protected wilderness area in the Maritimes. The Tobeatic Game Sanctuary is a 142,000 hectare area in the centre of the southwestern part of the province. Many other protected areas have followed, but the Tobeatic is one of the earliest attempts made in the Maritimes to protect a large tract of our wilderness.

✣ Birds that could eat like a horse ✣

Maritimers are quite familiar with the common house sparrow, but the tiny bird is not native to this region. It was probably introduced from Europe sometime in the 1850s and rapidly grew in population. But according to famed naturalist Robie Tufts, the number of house sparrows began to decline at the end of the nineteenth century, at the same time that automobiles replaced horses. The horses, in their own way, had supplied the sparrows with a food source with the spilled grains from their feed bags, and the undigested grains in their droppings. Less horse poop—fewer house sparrows.

☀ A sign of things to come ❖

Air and sewage pollution is nothing new to Halifax and its environs. In 1896, a gas works opened on the shores of the Northwest Arm near Point Pleasant Park. It was very unpopular with residents because it put noxious fumes in the air. In fact, the fumes were so bad that the gases killed trees in Point Pleasant Park, and the sewage pollution fouled the waters of the Arm. Local residents, who developed rashes and boils, had to sleep with their windows closed. By 1902, the gas works had ceased.

☀ Wood turtles welcome ❖

In 2006, when Shirley Cameron of Sherbrooke, Nova Scotia, donated a thirty-nine hectare section of watershed land along the St. Mary's River to the Nova Scotia Nature Trust, she and her family made a significant contribution to saving a unique natural habitat in Maritime Canada. What makes this donation so important is that this area is home to North America's largest population of wood turtles. Local and international efforts have gone into protecting this species of turtle, and saving their habitat will help the wood turtle stand a better chance of being around for a long time.

☀ UN approval for Nova Scotia wilderness ❖

Draw a line through Nova Scotia from the Bay of Fundy to Chester—the southwest portion of the province is a unique area in the Maritimes. In 2001, the United Nations Educational, Scientific and Cultural Organization (UNESCO) gave this area the designation of a unique biosphere reserve in recognition of its biodiversity and rich cultural heritage. The Southwest Nova Biosphere Reserve is the largest protected wilderness area in the Maritimes.

CHAPTER TWO

MARITIMERS

✦ Digging up the past ✦

Archaeological digs at St. Peters Canal on Cape Breton Island have found evidence of very early pre-contact inhabitants, possibly the ancestors of modern Mi'kmaq. There have been many digs throughout the Maritimes that have helped us learn more about the life of the region's first peoples. Sites at Dartmouth, Yarmouth, and Amherst Shore in Nova Scotia; Quaco Head, Kingsclear, and Hogan-Mullin in New Brunswick; and Souris in Prince Edward Island show evidence of past habitation, although not all scientists agree on who these early peoples were. The oldest of these sites is the one at Debert, Nova Scotia. Excavated in the 1960s under the direction of archaeologist George MacDonald, the site, believed to be a seasonal encampment near an ancient caribou trail, has been carbon dated to a period about 10,600 years ago.

✦ A polar pilot ✦

Canada's Royal Canadian Naval Air Service was established in 1918, and one of its first stations was in Dartmouth. Few Canadian pilots had received training. To help with this effort and provide a base for American navy pilots, the United States government sent planes and pilot instructors to assist in providing convoy air protection. One of those American pilots stationed at Dartmouth was Richard E. Bird—who later became a famed polar aviator and Antarctic explorer.

✦ A glowing recommendation ✦

In 1749, London blacksmith George Hicks travelled with Edward Cornwallis to help found Halifax. Here is a portion of a letter written home to his wife: "My dear, I live as well as a man can desire, I want for no money nor clothes, I want for no victuals nor drink, nor lodging, I want for nothing but you and my dear children, and should be very glad that you would come in the fleet, the next spring in the year '50; you shall be kindly welcome to enjoy my prosperous labour, as you may live an easy life, without labour to toil yourself."

❖ *Chinese Islanders* sets the record straight ❖

Historians once believed that the first Chinese citizens of Atlantic Canada were the thirty-five iron workers who came to Woodstock, New Brunswick, in 1880. But thanks to research carried out by Hung-Min Chiang for his book *Chinese Islanders*, we now know that the first person of Chinese decent to come to this region was Louisa Maria Hooper, a Chinese Portuguese native of the South China Portuguese colony of Macao. Louisa married William Hooper, and came to Prince Edward Island with her husband and family after he retired from government service in 1850.

❖ An idea in motion ❖

Walter Callow, a native of Parrsboro, Nova Scotia, was born in 1894, and during air training in World War One, was injured and eventually left a quadriplegic. Several years later, he went blind, but this amazing man forged on from his permanent bed at Camp Hill Hospital in Halifax to establish a bus service for those with disabilities. The first Walter Callow bus service began in 1948, and is still in operation today.

❖ A wave of war brides ❖

Canada has always been a nation of immigrants. Together with the First Nations people, the various ethnic and cultural groups living here make our three Maritime provinces a wonderfully rich mosaic of people and ideas. But, one statistic may surprise you—when you combine the approximately twenty-two thousand children who accompanied their war-bride mothers to this country after World War Two, you have the largest wave of immigrants to Canada in the twentieth century. The story of Canada's war brides is movingly told at Halifax's Pier 21 National Historic Site. Known as the Gateway to Canada, Pier 21 was Canada's "front door" to immigrants between the years of 1928 and 1971.

⤜ The first of the First Nations ⤛

The area today known as Canada's Maritime provinces was once primarily inhabited by two distinct nations—the Mi'kmaq and the Maliseet. Present-day New England's Passamaquoddy people covered a small portion of our modern Maritime provinces area, but the Mi'kmaq occupied the majority of the region. The lands around the western area of present-day New Brunswick up to the Miramichi region, and including the present St. John River system, were Maliseet territory. These two major nations lived, for the most part, in harmony, but shared a common enemy to their northern border—the Mohawk, who would occasionally send raiding parties into Mi'kmaq and Maliseet territories.

⤜ An ancestry of French convicts? ⤛

If initial attempts to colonize our region hadn't failed, many of us would be looking back to an ancestry of French convicts. That was who made up the band of settlers that arrived on Sable Island with the Marquis de la Roche in 1598. The sixty colonists were mostly escaping prison terms and death. Only twelve souls survived the first winter. Although the band was supplemented with additional settlers and eked out an existence for a few years, they gave up attempts at permanent settlement by 1602, after the exasperated band of settlers killed their leaders, and de la Roche was stripped of his title. Tenacity ruled, and the French eventually established the first permanent settlement in the Maritimes in 1604 at the mouth of the St. Croix River on St. Croix Island. In 1605, the settlers relocated to a better site at Port Royal.

✶ Devotion to Scouting ✦

Walter Wood of Kentville, Nova Scotia, devoted his life to working with young people, and for over half a century, worked to help Boy Scouting in the Maritimes. In 1978, at the age of 101, he was the oldest registered Scouter in the British Commonwealth, and in that same year, was awarded the Order of Canada. Wood was the oldest Canadian ever invested with that honour. Mr. Wood died in 1983—a remarkable Canadian and an outstanding Scout.

A name change ✶ for New Brunswick's ✦ largest river

For several thousand years, the First Nations people of the eastern seaboard used the large inland waterway leading into what we now call New Brunswick. Today's maps show that waterway as the St. John River, but before European settlement, the Maliseet and Mi'kmaq who hunted, fished, and grew corn and squash along its shores, called the river the Woolastook.

✶ Who was Nicholas Denys? ✦

One of the best-known early French settlers to Acadia was the adventurer and writer Nicholas Denys. He is known as a cartographer, settler, opportunist, speculator, and public servant. He served as Lieutenant-Governor of the area known today as the Maritime provinces, Newfoundland, and parts of the Gaspé. His work in the cod fishery and fur industry failed to make him the fortune he desired, and he returned to France in poverty. But he managed to come back to his beloved Acadia, and settled and died in the Baie des Chaleurs area of New Brunswick. His major work, published in 1672, was titled *The Description and Natural History of the Coasts of North America*. It continues to be one of the best records of early French and Mi'kmaq life in the new world.

❧ Love triumphs over all ❧

That was certainly the case for eighteenth-century Halifax lovers Aldolphus Christoph Vieth and Anna Dorothea Behm. Young Vieth was a German lieutenant serving in Halifax in the regiment of Baron Von Seitz. Lieutenant Vieth fell in love with Miss Behm, the daughter of a local German settler, and the couple were united in marriage. However, since the lieutenant didn't get permission from the Baron, he was arrested and his rank was reduced. The good news is that the marriage was a success. The couple had several children, and Mr. Vieth eventually inherited a German noble title.

❧ Denmark's North American home ❧

New Denmark, New Brunswick, is said to be the largest Danish colony in North America. The first immigrants arrived in 1872 and found themselves, as one historian wrote, "like children abandoned in the merciless woods." But those early Danish settlers survived even though times were so hard at the beginning, they were forced to dig their seed potatoes out of the ground and eat them to prevent starvation.

❧ Hardship follows immigrants ❧

Reverend John Wiswall kept a detailed journal while living among and preaching to the people of the Aylesford region of Nova Scotia in the 1790s. He wrote: "This part of the province is very thinly settled by persons of all descriptions in general extremely poor & scattered over the country in all directions, they chiefly live in Hutts [sic] little if anything superior to the Cabins in Ireland."

❧ Putting down roots in the Maritimes ❧

The Maritime Provinces of Canada were once solely inhabited by the First Nations peoples. But, with the introduction of Old World settlers, these demographics changed dramatically. In Prince Edward Island, about 75 percent of the present population is of Scottish and Irish origin. New Brunswick is Canada's only officially bilingual province, and at 35 percent, it has the highest percentage of francophones outside Quebec. The founders of New Brunswick were, for the most part, French, British Loyalist, Celtic, and Aboriginal, and later included German, Scandinavian, and Asian immigrants. In Nova Scotia, Mi'kmaq were the pre-contact peoples, and then came what many call the other five founding Old World cultures: French, English, African, Germanic and Celtic. All three Maritime provinces now also boast people from every part of the world—we are becoming a truly global community.

⤳ Strange visions ⤶

Nineteenth-century Baptist minister Silas Rand, collected and wrote down much of the earliest known Mi'kmaq lore and legends. An account he collected from Mi'kmaq Josiah Jeremy, tells of an early Mi'kmaq sighting of Europeans in the Maritimes. Mr. Jeremy told of a young girl who, in a strange dream, saw a small island floating toward the land. On this island were tall trees on which moved living beings. Mr. Jeremy said: "The next day an event occurred that explained all. What should they see but a singular little island…which had drifted near to the land…there were trees on it and branches to the trees, on which a number of bears…were crawling about…What was their surprise to find that these supposed bears were men."

⤳ Lebanese legacy ⤶

The Lebanese community in the Maritimes began with immigrants arriving in the mid-to-late 1800s. Many of those early arrivals worked as peddlers who established wide-ranging routes and a loyal and dedicated following. The first record of a Lebanese population on Prince Edward Island was in 1888. Almost one hundred years later, Joe Ghiz, who served as premier of Prince Edward Island from 1986 to 1993, became Canada's first provincial premier of Lebanese ancestry. In fact, Mr. Ghiz was the first premier in Canada of non-European ancestry. In 2007, Robert Ghiz followed in his father's political footsteps and became Prince Edward Island's premier.

Born in Nova Scotia, Edward Francis Arab, a second-generation Canadian of Lebanese heritage was a distinguished and compassionate lawyer, an early advocate for human rights, and a war hero. Sadly, in 1944 at the age of twenty-nine, Edward lost his life fighting in Holland. One of his most empowering legacies is his work to help found the Canadian Lebanese Society and become its first president in 1938.

⤳ Letters from the Maritimes ⤶

Do you wonder why anyone ever immigrated to this country, given some of the letters sent home by new arrivals to Canada? Take, for example, this August 1772 observation sent by James Metcalf in Maccan, Nova Scotia, to Ann Gill in England: "There is a little fly called the mosquito that is troublesome in summer time and bites like a midge but…it is becoming fewer because of land clearing and grazing. Sometimes we make smoke at our doorways in the evenings to keep the mosquitoes out—they are more troublesome than you can imagine."

Folklorist Helen Creighton says descendants of the German settlers who came to Nova Scotia's Lunenburg County in the 1750s told her the following: "They used to get letters from home but they never answered them…They thought if they'd write back and say it was so hard, why, the people'd say they had no business to come over there, and if they said it was good, others might come. They had terrible hard times."

⤳ Legend of the Maliseet Nation ⤶

According to First Nations' lore, the Maliseet nation grew out of the Mi'kmaq spiritual leader Kluscap's intervention. In ancient times, before there was a Maliseet nation, the Mi'kmaq and Mohawk were great enemies. One time, the Mi'kmaq repelled a Mohawk raid and captured some of the Mohawk women and children. Kluscap ordered the captives returned to their lands unharmed, but some of the warriors disobeyed and took the women as their wives. Legend says that Kluscap was so angered he expelled these warriors from the Mi'kmaq Confederacy, and these exiles became the progenitors of the Maliseet nation who settled along the shores of the St. John River.

⇢ New Brunswick's Chinese Canadians ⇠

By the 1890s, Saint John became home to the first trickle of Chinese immigrants to New Brunswick, and by the early 1900s, Saint John was the site of New Brunswick's largest Chinese community. Wing Hem immigrated to New Brunswick from China perhaps as early as 1911. His wife, Lim, also came from China and together they raised several children in China and Saint John. When their youngest son, Percy, was born in 1914, he became the first Chinese Canadian born in New Brunswick.

⇢ The Vatican and the Mi'kmaq ⇠

One of the earliest treaties between two sovereign states in what is now Canada took place in 1610 when the Vatican signed a treaty with Mi'kmaq leaders. It is known as the Mi'kmaq Concordat. The Mi'kmaq agreed to allow Catholic priests to build churches and introduce Christianity, and also promised to protect French settlers. In return, the Vatican recognized the status of the Mi'kmaq Nation as a sovereign authority.

⇢ Adventure and education ⇠

One of the earliest written accounts of Maliseet and French life in Canada is by New Englander John Gyles. In 1689 at the age of nine, John was abducted from his home by a Maliseet raiding party. He was later traded to a French family at Jemseg (in present-day New Brunswick), and eventually earned his freedom by helping save a French seigneur from an English raiding party. He returned to his New England home and wrote of his time with the Acadians and Maliseet. He had learned much about their language and customs, and eventually put his knowledge to use as a British officer in New England.

✦ A mosaic of Maritime ancestry ✦

The Canadian census for 1871 lists some very interesting statistics about the ethnic origins of the inhabitants of the Eastern Shore of Nova Scotia. Slightly over 22 percent listed their ethnicity as English; 15 percent as French, and slightly lower as Scottish; 12 percent Irish; a bit over 5 percent Black, and 2 percent Indian. What may seem surprising, until you remember the large number of so-called 'foreign protestants' residing in the province at the time, is that a full 25 percent—one quarter of the inhabitants—listed their ethnic origins as German. This makes sense when you realize that the foreign protestants were mainly non-Catholic, German-speaking settlers brought to the colony between 1750 and 1752. To make things confusing to future genealogists is that even as late as 1911, folks like my Croft ancestors in Guysborough County, Nova Scotia (who came to Halifax in 1750 as Jacob Kraft and family) were listed as Dutch, a then common term for folks of German (Deutsch) ancestry.

CHAPTER THREE

SEX, POLITICS, AND RELIGION

⟿ A prime minister buried abroad ⟾

Richard Bedford Bennett holds the distinction of being the only New Brunswick native to rise to the position of Canada's prime minister, serving from 1930 to 1935. His tenure was during the Great Depression, and his political legacy suffered as a result. Cars, pulled by animals because the owners couldn't afford gas, became known as Bennett Buggies. However, he often answered letters with financial aid from his own pocket. In 1939, after a bitter political defeat, he retired to England. It was there he died and was buried, earning him another distinction—the only Canadian prime minister not buried in Canada.

⟿ A Canadian leading Britain? ⟾

In 1922, Andrew Bonar Law was elected the prime minister of Britain. Sadly, due to ill health, he resigned in less than a year, died in 1923, and was buried in Westminster Abbey. What makes this statesman so unique is that he was the only British prime minister not born in the British Isles. Andrew Bonar Law was born in 1858 in Rexton, New Brunswick.

⟿ Canada's first Baptist congregation ⟾

Baptist congregations have a strong and loyal following in many Maritime communities. In 1776, the Reverend Nathan Mason led his Baptist followers from Swansea, Massachusetts to establish a religious community in Sackville, New Brunswick. Those pioneers are considered the first Baptist congregation in Canada.

⇥ Annapolis Royal, Maritime capital ⇤

Halifax, the largest city in Atlantic Canada, is the capital of Nova Scotia, but it didn't always hold its capital distinction. In 1710, thirty-nine years before the British established a settlement at Halifax, they captured Port Royal from the French and renamed it after Queen Anne, calling it Annapolis Royal. That town remained the colony's capital until Halifax was given the honour in 1749. Since this was all before the time when New Brunswick became a separate colony, and Prince Edward Island was still considered part of Nova Scotia, that would make Annapolis Royal the one-time capital of the Maritimes.

⇥ Lottery for Island land ⇤

In 1767, the British, who claimed ownership of Prince Edward Island, came up with a plan to increase the number of settlements—and make some cash on the side. They hatched a scheme to divide the Island into counties, parishes, and sixty-seven lots. The property would be owned by absentee landlords, and Islanders would be nothing more than tenants on land owned by folks living in Britain. On July 23, 1767, a lottery to determine land ownership was held in Britain. Names were pulled from a hat and the Island was divvied up.

The Island obtained a form of colonial government in 1769, but lacked the right to levy taxes on land owners. Although other provinces had settlers who owned land either through land grants or purchase, Prince Edward Island's settlers lived on land owned either by the Crown or by absentee landlords who were granted the lands in the lottery of 1767. Many of these land owners failed to live up to their obligation of bringing settlers to the Island or paying rents for the lands. It wasn't until 1832 that the Island colony gained the right to tax properties in order to make local improvements.

⇥ Got religion? ⇤

The eighteenth century was a time of religious change and conflict in the Maritimes. The Mi'kmaq had, for the most part, adopted the Catholic religion of their French allies yet maintained their deep, pre-contact spiritual affiliation. Catholics were relegated to the status of second-class citizens, and the evangelical New Light Movement, introduced in 1775 by the charismatic preacher, Henry Alline, spread fervent Protestantism across the Maritimes.

⇥ Presumptuous papists ⇤

During the colonial period, being an adherent of any religion other than the Church of England meant you could expect little in the line of political or social advancement in the Maritimes. The Education Act of 1766 clearly stated, "if any popish recusant, papist or person professing the popish religion, shall be so presumptive as to set up any school within this province, and be detected therein, such offender shall, for every such offence, suffer three months' imprisonment without mainprize [bail]...and shall pay a fine to the King of ten pounds."

⇥ Have altar, will travel ⇤

In 1790, a young Catholic priest named Father John MacEachern emigrated from Scotland to St. John's Island—known today as Prince Edward Island. Since he spoke Gaelic, his superiors in Quebec also gave him the charge of Cape Breton Island and parts of northern Nova Scotia. His territory was so large that he often travelled by canoe or coastal sailing vessels. In winter, Father John devised a portable altar housed in a small boat that had runners on the sides, making the altar a combination of a sled and a boat.

⇥ A very expensive sermon ⇤

Sometimes taking a political stand can cost you dearly. When St. Matthew's Church was established in Halifax in the mid-eighteenth century, the government granted an additional twenty-seven hectares of land between Oxford Street and the Northwest Arm to the church. However, those lands were taken back in 1785 when the church's minister preached a sermon in support of the colonists fighting the American Revolution to the south. Today, that land would be worth a fortune, and so it's been said to be one of the most expensive sermons ever preached.

⇥ Mussel shells for mortar ⇤

Consecrated in 1790, St. Mary's Church in Auburn, Nova Scotia, is one of the oldest Anglican churches in North America. The church's history goes back to the time of the Loyalists. This lovely little church also has two other identities. It is known as The Little Wren Church, so named because it is constructed along the lines of Sir Christopher Wren's English church designs of the Georgian era. It is also called Mussel Shell Church. Legend has it that starving Acadian deportees, suffering a most gruelling winter at Morden, left mounds of mussel shells at the shore. These were later found and powdered into a substitute mortar when the Loyalist church builders found themselves short of lime.

⇥ Battle for the border ⇤

The Madawaska region of Maine and New Brunswick was once a hotly contested piece of real estate. The area was mainly settled by exiled Acadians returning home, but the United States and Britain could not agree on the boundary—it bisected the settlers' domain. In 1827, a boundary dispute threatened peace between the two nations, and in 1837, this squabbling escalated into what became known as the Aroostook War. Troops were called in from both camps, and after some brawls and taking of prisoners, the border dispute was resolved and the international border finalized. The losers were the inhabitants of Madawaska, who found their homeland now straddling the United States and Canada.

⤚ A very public break-up ⤙

The press can be a powerful medium. Publishing your personal business can sometimes work for you, but it can also work against you. Take this example of a couple advertising their differences in the *Kentville Advertiser* in 1973. I'll omit the last name in case the couple happens to be back together. The first ad came from the man, Henry: "My wife, Julia left my bed and board ten months ago. I will not be responsible for any bills in my name contracted by her." The wife's notice followed shortly after: "In answer to last week's notice, I, Julia, did not leave my husband's bed and board, I was kicked out. I own the bed and I've fed myself as he has never worked during the last five years since I married him."

You might call this couple the ultimate Valentine's Day born losers. From the *Halifax Herald* for February 14, 1899, comes this sad announcement: "William Johnson, who was arrested yesterday on a charge of stealing iron from Alderman McFatridge, was to have been married today. It is likely that the ceremony will have to be postponed owing to his present difficulties."

⤚ Profanity in the churchyard ⤙

We often think of early Maritime Christians as solemn churchgoers—dour and respectable. But maybe we should take into account this comment written about Prince Edward Island Scots attending their church in the late eighteenth century: "Before and after Mass they were in the habit of talking as freely as they would in a profane place. They also allowed their dogs to enter the church and run around as if they were in the houses of their masters." The author also noted "the immodesty of the women, who came to the sacraments with their throats exposed to a degree that should not allow them even to enter the church."

❖ Nova Scotia's first premier: princely or pompous? ❖

The first person to hold the title of premier of Nova Scotia was James Boyle Uniacke. He took office on February 2, 1848. Folks of the day either loved him or loathed him. One of his contemporaries described him as "the aristocrat…tall, graceful, and a 'prince among men'…always attired in the latest London fashion." A less-friendly contemporary, perhaps commenting on Mr. Uniacke's reputation for drinking and womanizing, called him "a pompous piece of perishable clay!"

❖ Preston's legacy ❖

Cornwallis Street Baptist Church in Halifax has been serving the African Nova Scotian community since the 1830s. Richard Preston, an escaped slave from Virginia who worked on behalf of the Baptist mission in Nova Scotia, secured funds from the West London Baptist Association in England. The church was also helped along by a donation from the provincial House of Assembly. Once it was constructed, Reverend Preston served the Cornwallis Street Baptist Church as its pastor for thirty years.

❖ Violent voting in early elections ❖

Elections in the Maritimes can be nasty things; however, today's mud-slinging and backstabbing pale in comparison to some of the violent acts brought about by election fervour among our earlier political rivals. One such example is the election held in New Brunswick in 1843 in the Miramichi region. The contest pitted timber barons Alexander Rankin and his ally, John Street, against their mutual rival, Joseph Cunard. This was no gentlemen's contest. Factions for both sides fought with zeal, and resorted to such violence that at times gangs of between five hundred and a thousand converged on polling stations in an attempt to deny their rivals the right to vote. It grew so bad that one man was killed. Troops were eventually called in to quell the storm and Cunard went down in defeat.

⤳ Rummies and Smashers ⤶

Nicknames can often tell more about a cause than hard facts. For example, during the temperance movement in New Brunswick in the mid-nineteenth century, those opposed to liquor were known as Smashers for their wont to destroy stills and other spirit-manufacturing devices. Their opponents, those in favour of allowing moderate and responsible drinking, went by the moniker Rummies.

⤳ Political criticism—in verse ⤶

Biting political commentary is nothing new to readers of Maritime newspapers. In fact, in the nineteenth century, some political wits could be downright caustic. William Craig was a Halifax resident who regularly contributed his political opinions to the local papers, and self-published his own social commentary in verse. One interesting example is when he shows his great displeasure at Joseph Howe's change from anti-Confederate spokesman to a member of Sir John A. Macdonald's cabinet. In 1869, Mr Craig versed his disgust at Howe with these lines:

> What has come o'er our champion Joe,
> That he has been converted so,
> Why should he go and join the foe,
> Go with the traitors one and a',
> You've sold yourself to Ottawa.

⤳ Who was Canada's longest-serving provincial premier? ⤶

Elected as Nova Scotia's premier in 1896, George H. Murray served in that office for twenty-seven years, making him Nova Scotia's, and Canada's, longest-serving provincial premier. Under his leadership, his province saw the introduction of the vote for women, and workers' compensation. He twice declined a knighthood and retired from office in 1923.

⟶ Incentive to drink a glass of wine ⟵

Here's an interesting idea used by the province of Nova Scotia in 1808 for funding a pension for a retiring government employee. In that year, when Sir John Wentworth retired as lieutenant-governor of Nova Scotia, he was granted an annual lifetime pension of five hundred pounds. And where did the province find the pension funds? The money was raised by taxing an additional six pence per gallon on all wines imported into the province.

⟶ Sylvia Pankhurst in the Maritimes? ⟵

Each time an election rolls around, Canadians are admonished to get out and vote. While some folks take voting for granted, there are Maritime Canadian women voting even now who remember an era when they didn't have that right. Women were granted the federal vote in Canada in 1917 (subject to restrictions and conditions). Nova Scotia followed that same year; New Brunswick came on board in 1919, and Prince Edward Island granted women the franchise in 1922. In New Brunswick, although women could vote, they were not allowed to run for public office until 1934.

Although New Brunswick women couldn't vote in provincial elections until 1919 and federal elections until 1921, some early champions of women's rights did make their voices heard. In the 1890s, the Saint John Women's Enfranchisement Association was formed, and in 1912, this organization sponsored the visit of famed British suffragist, Sylvia Pankhurst.

⊹ **When is a city a city?** ⊹

In 1845, Fredericton had four thousand inhabitants. To qualify for city status, it needed a population of ten thousand. But the Church of England needed a bishopry in New Brunswick, and bishopries needed to be based in a city. Since Fredericton was the capital of New Brunswick, Queen Victoria, the head of the British church, made a decree that Fredericton be given city status. So how do you really know that a city is a city? When the Queen says so!

✐ CHAPTER FOUR ✐
ART, LITERATURE, AND LEISURE

✦ Celtic competition on Prince Edward Island ✦

Celtic heritage was nurtured early in Maritime history. On August 17, 1864, the first annual gathering of the Caledonia Club in Prince Edward Island was held on the grounds of Government House. It held competitions and awarded cash prizes in such Scottish events as Gaelic poetry, proficiency in Highland pipe music, putting the stone, sword dances, the long leap, running foot and hurdle races, and tossing the caber. There was also a thirty-shilling prize for the best Highland costume of Island manufacture.

✦ Using wit and pen to comment on Maritime life ✦

Robert Chambers, a native of Wolfville, Nova Scotia, was a respected illustrator and cartoonist when he took on the job of staff editorial cartoonist with the *Halifax Herald* in the 1930s. For forty years, Bob Chambers commented on life in the Maritimes, using his wit and his pen. His social and political cartoons rang true with Maritime sentiment, and his beloved "Everyman" character came to represent the average Maritimer in so many ways.

✦ The Windsor Ex ✦

On May 21, 1765, the first regular agricultural exhibition in what would become Canada was held in Nova Scotia. Established by an act of legislation, the exhibition was meant to draw attention to the English presence in the former Acadian community of Piziquid, newly renamed

Windsor. Participants vied for a number of prizes in various categories including showing cattle and other animals, and displaying grains, dairy products, and homespun materials. Prizes included plowshares, saddles, whips, and spurs. In a running race, the winner received a medal and a pair of buckskin breeches, while winning wrestlers received shoes and buckles.

✧ The Island's most famous poet ✧

Prince Edward Island's most famous, and some might say infamous, poet was Milton Acorn. The Charlottetown native was born in 1923. Milton rose to join the ranks of Canada's most celebrated poets, eventually winning the Canadian Poets Award in 1970 and the Governor General's Award in 1975 for his work, *The Island Means Minago*. His social causes were legendary as was his unique personality, which didn't curry favour with many of his critics. He has been called "a troubadour of the working class", and is known on the Island as the "people's poet." Milton Acorn died in 1986, but his legend and his work continue to be recognized for their distinct Island qualities.

✧ Racing for a gold cup ✧

Horse racing has a long and colourful history in the Maritimes. Our Victorian ancestors enjoyed competitive matches such as the one held in 1840 in New Brunswick. The Bathurst Jockey Club held races against the Miramichi Turf Club and vied for a prized gold cup worth one hundred sovereigns.

✧ A party fit for a prince ✧

Eighteenth-century diarist, William Dyott, offered high praise for a party given aboard Prince William Henry's ship when he was in port at Halifax. "There were near fourteen ladies and thirty gentlemen. We danced till one o'clock. The ladies went below, and the colours that divided the quarter-deck were drawn...and displayed the most completely elegant supper I ever saw. Upwards to sixty people sat down to supper...chiefly cold, except soup and removes, with partridges, champagne, hock, etc. We danced till three o'clock, when the champagne began to operate with some of the gentlemen, and the ladies thought it near time to go on shore." The prince, who visited Halifax in 1786 and 1787 as captain of the HMS *Pegasus*, later became King William IV.

⤋ A medieval castle made for moviegoers ⤉

In the heady days of the 1920s, '30s, and '40s, many movie theatres were built to resemble grand palaces or fantasy castles. One of the most famous and beloved of these over-the-top edifices in the Maritimes was the Capital Theatre in Halifax. Designed by Toronto architect Murray Brown, the medieval castle-inspired theatre opened for business in 1930. It housed live performances, as well as regular showings of the popular movies of the day. Its interior was covered with murals; walkways resembled moats and drawbridges; and it even boasted a suit of armour. I well remember attending the dear old Capital and mourned its loss when it was torn down in 1974.

⤋ Hockey, Island style ⤉

While Prince Edward Island can't profess to being the birthplace of hockey (Nova Scotia claims that title), the Island has some interesting historical hockey data, too. The first men's hockey game on Prince Edward Island was held on February 7, 1890, when the Hillsborough Hockey Club staged an exhibition game. It ended in an 8–8 tie.

⤋ A strong argument against gambling ⤉

Sometime the rationale used against gambling is as controversial as gambling itself. The *Acadian Recorder* for December 20, 1817, carried a letter concerning gambling with playing cards in Halifax. The writer was most concerned with female gamblers: "Men, from their more liberal education, and the contact with the outside world, have a thousand opportunities of improving their minds, from which women are necessarily barred…a slate of society…which excludes conversation, and chains down the mind to painted figures on bits of paper, is hostile to intellectual expansion, and dooms the fairer sex of creation to frivolity and ignorance."

✦ The hat box manuscript ✦

Here's an amazing story about never giving up. In 1905, a first-time novelist penned a story she felt would be well-liked and sent it off to several publishers. They all rejected her book. Discouraged, the writer tucked the manuscript away in a hat box. In 1907, the author found the manuscript, and after reading it again, believed in her story enough to send it off to yet another publishing house. The Page Company of Boston liked her book. They published it in 1908, and the rest is history. That writer? Lucy Maud Montgomery. Her book? *Anne of Green Gables.*

If you're a fan of Lucy Maud Montgomery, you'll enjoy this bit of trivia about her dwelling places. Ms. Montgomery's birthplace on Prince Edward Island was in New London, and she lived for several years in Cavendish. But she also lived, as they say, off Island. On the corner of Barrington and Bishop streets in Halifax is a stone building erected in 1828, with the name Wallace Street inscribed in one of the sandstone blocks. That's the former name of Bishop Street. This stone dwelling is also the house where Ms. Montgomery boarded on the third floor while attending Dalhousie College. A fact even less well-known is that, in 1911, after her marriage to Ewan MacDonald, Lucy Maud moved permanently to the town of Leaskdale in—(gasp) Ontario!

✦ Private Ross Hamilton's alter ego ✦

The most famous Canadian entertainment troop during World War One was a music/comedy ensemble known as the Dumbells. Arguably, the most well-known and beloved member of the Dumbells was a character nicknamed Marjorie—a charming lass who was the alter ego of a young ambulance driver, Private Ross Hamilton. Born in Pugwash, Ross began impersonating Marjorie in 1917, and she became an instant hit with the doughboys. Ross and the Dumbells toured their show until 1932, and after retiring to his native province, he died in 1965.

↷ Good sports ↶

Guiding visiting hunters and anglers is still an important business for a handful of Maritimers. But in the nineteenth and early to mid-twentieth centuries, many people worked during the hunting and fishing season guiding those who could pay for the opportunity to come home with a prize. American businessmen and sports heroes were the main users of the guides' services and these men were always referred to as sports.

↷ A friendly foe ↶

The War of 1812 was the only official armed conflict between the United States and the Canadian colonies of Great Britain. One might have expected the area along the New Brunswick/American border to be a hotbed of strife, but this was not so. In fact, most New Englanders opposed the war and trade continued so that unarmed American vessels were still allowed into Saint John. And, how's this for friendly support? During the war the citizens of the St. Croix valley shared their supply of gunpowder with their neighbours in Calais so their American friends could properly celebrate the Fourth of July.

↷ Images of our past ↶

Many of the quintessential Maritime photographic images from our past are the work of Wallace and Elva Macaskill. A Macaskill photograph is a prized work of art and reproductions are still in high demand. Both Cape Breton natives, Wallace and Elva worked as a team, usually with

Wallace taking the photograph and Elva working her delicate magic to hand-tint each print.

✧ Charlottetown's winter wonderland ✦

In an 1832 report for the British government, John McGregor described some winter activities in Charlottetown: "The amusements of Charlotte Town, although not on so extensive a scale, are in imitation of those at Halifax. During winter, assemblies are usual, once a month, or oftener. An amateur theatre, very respectfully fitted up, affords an opportunity of spending some pleasant hours. Picnic Parties are common during summer and winter. The ice, during winter, frequently affords excellent skating. As the expense of keeping a horse is trifling, almost every housekeeper has one or two; and during winter, it is a favourite amusement among all classes to drive in cabrioles, which are slight open carriages set on runners, which slip easily and rapidly over the snow and ice."

✧ Our very own jazz legend ✦

Nova Scotia has produced some legendary jazz musicians. Take, for example, Cheticamp vibraphonist Warren Chaisson. In 1959, he headed to New York and worked with Dave Shearing, and that same year, he also made an appearance at the famous Newport Jazz Festival. In 1984, Warren won a Grammy Award for his album with B. B. King titled *Blues and Jazz*.

✧ The man who made the songs ✦

Larry Gorman was a nineteenth-century poet and songwriter from Prince Edward Island who became famous throughout the Maritimes and northern New England for his satirical and caustic songs and verses. One of Larry's favourite habits was to show up at mealtime—and any homemaker who didn't serve him a decent meal was liable to find herself lampooned in verse. Such was the case of two PEI lasses who were making a supper of porridge for their family and their guest, Larry, when a couple of handsome bachelors arrived unannounced. The meal plans were quickly altered as Larry's verse attests:

> Oh Lord be praised,
> I am amazed, how things can be amended;
> With cake and tea and such glee, when porridge was intended.

✣ The greatest show on earth ✣

For six summer days in 1864, Charlottetown was home to the Olympic Circus when it set up on a corner lot of Queen and Fitzroy streets. The circus boasted the most beautiful equestrians, the most daring acrobats, comical monkeys, a troop of acting dogs, and a trick horse named Pegasus. It was grandly announced that patrons could also see the Kremlin Marabouts, and promised that a troop of "Arab nomads of the desert" would appear every afternoon. The arrival of a circus in a Maritime town was a big event in the Victorian era, and people came from far away to enjoy the excitement. When the circus set up in Charlottetown, excursions were set up for parties to come by boat from Summerside, Shediac in New Brunswick, and Brule and Pictou in Nova Scotia.

✣ Trading tight boots for quiet scenes of nature ✣

Young people can never hope to please their elders. The odd thing is, it was that way when I was a kid, and I suppose, for every generation before me. In 1865, Andrew Downs, who operated the first zoo in North America from his home near the Dutch Village Road in Halifax, once advised young men of that city "to take more interest than they do in the natural history of their country." He also advised that "many an hour passed in walking up and down Granville Street in tight boots might be devoted far more profitably to studying the quiet scenes of nature."

→ A perfect day for a pin-nic ←

The following ad was placed in the Charlottetown papers of June 20, 1864: "The annual pin-nic of the Benevolent Irish Society will be held at Warre's Farm on Monday. The Steamer *Heather Belle* has been engaged for the day...leaving Pownal's Wharf. Violinists have been engaged for the attendance. No one but the persons authorized will be allowed to sell liqueurs or refreshments on the grounds."

→ A Wilde reputation ←

The great Irish social commentator and playwright, Oscar Wilde, arrived in Halifax in 1882 to begin his North American speaking tour. His reputation as a man with a razor-sharp wit who delivered lightning-fast comebacks didn't disappoint, for when he was asked at Halifax customs if he had anything to declare, he replied, "Only my genius!" Mr. Wilde's reputation had preceded him—some loved him, others loathed him. His lectures at the Academy of Music were packed, but the Halifax paper, *Presbyterian Witness*, declared Mr. Wilde was "not a decent associate in any society."

→ For men only ←

While lauding the features of the Waegwoltic Club in his 1908 publication *Sketches and Traditions of the Northwest Arm*, John Regan wrote: "In winter the club will be useful to citizens who are members as a pleasant place to have skating or card parties and dancing. Musical concerts and smokers promise to be very attractive." Most of those choices for winter entertainment are obvious to us today, but you may well ask, what was a smoker? Today, we may call it a stag party—not the sometimes raucous affair that may precede weddings, but simply a party considered suitable only for men.

✦ Devil's Island Easter ✦

I wonder how many celebrants shared this Easter custom with the residents of Devil's Island (at the mouth of Halifax Harbour), as remembered by my friend, Sister Sadie Henneberry: "Each family on the Island had an Easter Table. We received an Easter goodie. It might have been a chocolate bunny, rooster, chicken or marshmallow egg. All the rest was put on the Easter Table. This table was completely covered with coloured straw and then filled with coloured jellybeans, Easter eggs, ornaments and egg cups. People went from house to house to see the Easter Table just as we do at Christmas to see the trees."

✦ An early end to World War One ✦

World War One officially ended on November 11, 1918. But residents of North Sydney, Nova Scotia, celebrated one day early. Seems a telegrapher working in the cable office decoded the news from Europe and let it leak a day before the official announcement. By early afternoon, the whole town knew and began celebrating. Schools and businesses shut down, the liquor store gave free samples, and the residents danced in the streets.

✦ A holiday in May ✦

The twenty-fourth of May used to be known as Arbor Day—once a popular springtime holiday when residents planted trees to enrich their communities. A letter to the editor of the *Charlottetown Patriot* attests to this the rich arboreal heritage. The writer stated: "The descendants of the Arbor Committee [will] bask under the shade of the trees planted this 24th day of May, 1884, and feel a grateful pride in the thought that their forebearers exercised so much care and forethought for their comfort and enjoyment."

The twenty-fourth of May was also the official birthday celebration of Victoria Maria Louisa of Saxe-Coburg (born in 1819), the woman who reigned as Queen Victoria and whose name is most often associated with the nineteenth century—the Victorian Age. A popular rhyme that lasts even today in some Maritime circles said: "The twenty-fourth of May is the Queen's birthday; If we don't get a holiday we'll all run away."

⊹ Colleen Jones: a household name ⊱

Halifax native Colleen Jones is without question the most successful female curler in Canada. She won her first Nova Scotia curling title at age nineteen, and in 1982, became the youngest competitor to win the Canadian Ladies Curling Championship. Colleen led her 2001 team to win the World Curling Championship in Switzerland, and they continued to shine, capping off a new record at the 2004 Tournament of Hearts, to give Colleen and her team four straight Canadian titles. A member of the Canadian Curling Hall of Fame, Colleen is also known throughout the nation as an accomplished sports commentator and CBC Television weather personality.

The world's first periodical devoted to the sport of curling, aptly titled *The Curler*, was issued by the Halifax Curling Club in 1931. Incidentally, that club is the third oldest curling club in the nation behind clubs in Montreal and Quebec.

⊹ A top secret chess match ⊱

The undersea telegraph cable office in North Sydney, Cape Breton, was North America's connection with Europe for decades, and played a very important and serious role in transatlantic communications. But there were lighter moments in the office, too. During World War Two, the operators set up a chessboard so they could follow along with a trans-atlantic game played between Winston Churchill, prime minister of England, and Franklin Roosevelt, president of the United States, that was transmitted using a secret code.

⋄ Canada's first novelist a teenager? ⋄

The first novel written by a Canadian-born writer was penned by a teenager. It was an adventure novel titled *Saint Ursula's Convent*, written by a seventeen-year-old New Brunswick girl in 1803. Still, it wasn't published until twenty years later, and even then, the author's identity remained unknown until after her death in 1867. Julia Catherine Beckwith Hart was born in Fredericton in 1796. She later moved to Kingston, Ontario where two hundred copies of her book were published anonymously. *Saint Ursula's Convent* is a melodramatic novel of shipwrecks and family adventures. The book and the identity of its author were almost lost until mention of it was published in W. G. MacFarlane's *New Brunswick Bibliography* in 1895. Today, Julia Catherine Beckwith Hart is known as Canada's first native-born novelist.

⋄ The prime minister of the blues ⋄

The East Coast Music Awards (ECMAs) celebrations have become the pinnacle event for the Maritime music industry. The first recipient of the ECMAs Lifetime Achievement Award was "Canada's Prime Minister of the Blues," Dutch "Dutchy" Mason. In his 1989 acceptance speech, Dutchy reminded people, "If they keep having awards like this, people from all over will have to come and listen. That makes sense and sooner or later it will make dollars and sense." Dutch Mason, who died in 2007, was truly a prophet in his own time.

In 1991, the ECMAs Lifetime Achievement Award was renamed the Dr. Helen Creighton Lifetime Achievement Award in recognition of my late mentor's pioneering work in preserving the traditional music of Maritime Canada. I was honoured to accept the award in Helen's memory.

⁂ Christmas in the navy ⁂

Christmas for the men serving in Canada's navy during World War Two often introduced strange customs to the new sailors. The youngest rating on board donned the captain's uniform and became ruler of the ship for Christmas day. He fared better than the poor captain who, with his officers, had to make the rounds of every mess in the ship, offering Christmas tidings to the crew. The captain was expected to have a drink at every mess—and a battleship could have forty or fifty messes. Mess decks were decorated with greenery and coloured paper, or whatever was at hand. However, the centrepiece of the shipboard decorations was a large loaf of bread, pinned to the mess table with a bayonet. The bread was accompanied by a sign reading, "The staff of life, at the point of death." It was a grim reminder of the perils of war, despite the holiday.

⁂ Dressing like a gentleman ⁂

Gentlemen today rarely wear shirts and stiff collars with ties when they don't have to. But, in my grandfather's day, even farmers and fishermen would get spit-polished to come to town and shop for groceries on a Friday evening. Men also wore ties and vests while sportfishing and hunting. And, in the nineteenth and early twentieth centuries, for the fellows who couldn't afford stiff linen collars that needed constant washing and starching, there were inexpensive paper collars that would do the trick.

Gentlemen looking to upgrade their Christmas wardrobe in Charlottetown in 1863 had to look no further than Bell's Clothing Store. In December, they offered "the latest styles in Black, Blue and Brown West of England Broad Cloths, Beaver, Whitney, Tweeds, Doeskins, Vestings and a general assortment of Tailor's Trimmings." Mr. Bell also offered socks, braces, underclothing, and a selection of fancy flannel in red and white.

⇥ The Maritimes' music man ⇤

Richard Bulkeley came to Halifax in 1749 as aide-de-camp to Governor Edward Cornwallis. He was a wealthy, highly cultivated Irishman who eventually became provincial secretary and judge of the vice-admiralty court. Richard purchased land almost immediately upon arriving in the new town, and before beginning construction on his house, he chartered a vessel for Louisbourg to bring back cut stone from the ruins for its foundation. That stone still forms the lower level of his former residence, known today as Carleton House, Halifax's oldest residential building. Richard Bulkeley rose to become one of Halifax's most prominent citizens. He had many accomplishments both official and private, not the least of which was establishing a Pencil and Brush Club—probably the first artist's club formed in the New World. A man of great musical tastes, Richard was organist at St. Paul's Anglican Church, and according to the *Encyclopedia of Music in Canada*, he may also be considered "the father of music in English-speaking Canada."

Richard Bulkeley died in 1800, and is buried at his beloved St. Paul's Anglican Church, just across the street from his residence on the corner of Argyle and Prince streets.

⇥ Idleness, drinking, and gambling ⇤

Governments in the Maritimes have made efforts to control gambling practices for centuries. On June 19, 1779, the Government of Nova Scotia issued a proclamation against gaming tables, saying: "In spite of the law against public gambling, this practice continues whereby the fortunes of many have been ruined and the lives of many persons lost." But that wasn't the end of the argument. By 1786, horse racing was flourishing in Halifax and attempts were made to discontinue it because it was said to lead to idleness, drinking, and gambling.

✦ George Godfrey, heavyweight champ ✦

Charlottetown native George Godfrey was born in 1853 in the predominately African Canadian area known as The Bog, near the present residence of the lieutenant-governor. As a young man, George left the Island to work as a railway porter in Boston. While in that city, he started to train as a boxer at Professor Bailey's Hub City Gym, and at age twenty-six, began fighting competitively in the bare-knuckles tour. Boxing under the name Old Chocolate, George Godfrey fought in more than one hundred matches in every locale from music halls and boxing rings, and eventually won the World Coloured Heavyweight Championship. He died in 1901, an Island son and a sporting legend.

✦ A number-one lullaby ✦

In 1932, Wilf Carter from Port Hilford, Nova Scotia, recorded "My Swiss Lullabies" for RCA in Montreal. That song is considered the first hit recorded in Canada by a Canadian. Wilf became a famous cowboy singer, and he and I share a common influence. When he was a baby in Port Hilford, my great-grandmother Cora McDiarmid babysat him and sang him to sleep. Many years later, she did the same for me in nearby Sherbrooke. So I like to think Wilf and I got our musical start from the same lady.

✦ Longfellow and Acadia ✦

Henry Wadsworth Longfellow is the poet who, in 1847, immortalized the fictional Acadian lovers Evangeline and Gabriel. It is often said he wrote "Evangeline: A Tale of Arcadie" without ever setting foot on Acadian soil, but in truth, he was born and raised in Maine in a part of the state that was once ancient Acadian land. He also owned shares in a coal mine in Cape Breton, although he never visited his holdings there.

✦ Polo, the sport of kings and Haligonians ✦

Polo is known as the sport of kings, but it was also once the sport of Haligonians. Polo was introduced to Canada by officers of the 20th Regiment in 1878. Given the huge presence of the British military in nineteenth- and early-twentieth-century Halifax, polo must have been a popular game for many. In 1878, a polo club was established on grounds bordered by Chebucto Road, Monastery Lane, Quinpool Road, and Oxford Street today. In the 1880s, the land at Fort Needham was turned into a polo field for officers from nearby Wellington Barracks. The game's popularity waned with the decline of the British cavalry, and by 1893 it ceased to be played on any regular basis in Halifax.

✦ Belle of the Miramichi ball ✦

In Victorian New Brunswick, the belle of the ball was a social position that many vied for. Take this account of an 1861 Miramichi ball attended by sixteen-year-old Henrietta Hamill: "Henrietta wore a charming dress of pink tarlatan, low in the neck, little sleeves looped up with apple blossoms, a large corsage bouquet of the same. After supper [which consisted of cold turkey, ham, tongue, mashed potatoes…trifle and cakes of all sorts] the gentlemen retired, as was customary, to decide who was the belle of the ball. Henrietta in her pink dress was voted the belle."

✦ Buzz about a bee ✦

Back in the days when folks knew many old-time songs by heart, men (it was almost always men) would gather in a house or at the blacksmith's shop and have song contests. These feats of memory could often last three or four days, and would end when the last song remembered by any of the participants was sung. If no other song could be recalled by any of the singers, the final singer was champion of the singing bee.

⇾ A song to help the day go by ⇽

Here's a scene reminiscent of something in a Thomas Hardy novel. New Brunswick folk historian Louise Manny writes of interviewing workers who remembered going to the blueberry fields in hay wagons, and singing traditional songs throughout the day. She was told the songs not only passed the time, but served as sound signals for the children in case they strayed from the pickers.

⇾ A poem for the pioneer spirit ⇽

The first native-born English-language poet in Canada was Oliver Goldsmith, who published his poem, "The Rising Village" in 1825. Born in St. Andrews, New Brunswick, Oliver was the namesake of his great-uncle, the famed Anglo-Irish writer, Oliver Goldsmith. In "The Rising Village", which was modelled after his uncle's poem, "The Deserted Village", Oliver laments the loss of rural life while honouring the pioneer spirit of the new land. "The Rising Village" was first published in London, and then reprinted in Saint John by John McMillan.

⇾ Take me out to the Maritime ball game ⇽

Baseball has long been a popular sport in the Maritimes. In 1842, the Knickerbocker Baseball Club, the first formal American baseball team, was founded in New York City. Halifax and Saint John had baseball teams as early as 1838, and by 1873, four clubs were playing in Halifax. Players in the young men's social club wore knickers, jerseys, striped caps, and stockings. For hand protection, they wore simple fingerless leather gloves. When large padded gloves were introduced in the 1890s, one critic proclaimed: "Hundreds of men are playing...baseball now who aren't natural players. Take away those pillows and see how long they last." When Saint John native William Phillips, joined the Cleveland Blues in 1879, he became the first Canadian-born baseball player to play in the American major leagues.

☆ Imagine swimming with stockings on ☆

In the early part of the nineteenth century it was reported that one daring woman, competing in diving meets at Halifax's Waegwoltic Club on the Northwest Arm, decided to increase her chances of winning by removing her stockings before taking the plunge. It's not known whether she won or lost, but her activities were reported to the club's secretary, and her membership was suspended for two weeks.

☆ An early critic of the folk song ☆

The lumber camps of New Brunswick were one of the most important sources for the oral transmission of hundreds of traditional folk songs found in the Maritimes. Many of these songs were eventually compiled by Newcastle's town librarian, Louise Manning. However, not all visitors were so engaged by the wealth of folk songs. In 1811, British officer Lieutenant Colonel Joseph Gubbins was assigned to ready New Brunswick's militia against a possible attack from the Americans. His observations of New Brunswick life are caustic and elitist, and he once described hearing a collection of songs at a local singing party as "too bad to even laugh at."

☆ Faster, higher, stronger ☆

Charlottetown native Bill Halpenny, may be the most famous Canadian Olympic athlete never to win an Olympic medal. He had established the world record for the pole vault at the 1904 St. Louis World's Fair, so seemed a shoo-in for the title at the 1912 Stockholm Olympic Games; however, he wasn't permitted to compete because his pole didn't arrive on time for the Games. Halpenny believed he was still the best man, so when his pole did arrive several days later, he asked for and was granted the right to a demonstration vault. To prove his point, Halpenny asked that the bar be placed one inch higher than the recent Olympic winner's mark. He cleared it with ease! Sweden's king was so impressed that he ordered a special medal struck for Bill, which read: "To the greatest pole vaulter in the world."

The first Prince Edward Islander to win an Olympic medal was Bill MacMillan of Charlottetown, who brought home a bronze in hockey from the Grenoble Winter Olympics in 1968. J. Garfield MacDonald became Nova Scotia's first Olympic medal winner when he won a silver in the hop-step-jump competition at the 1908 games in London. New Brunswick's first Olympic medal came when Saint John speed skater William "Willie" Logan won two bronze medals at the 1932 Games in Lake Placid, New York.

On April 19, 1926, nineteen-year-old Johnny Miles, a Cape Breton coal miner, entered the famous Boston marathon and beat out all contenders, including both the reigning Olympic champion and the previous winner. He won the race again in 1929. Not only did he win twice, but held the record for fastest time until 1947. An annual running event is held at New Glasgow, Nova Scotia, in his honour—the Johnny Miles Marathon is a qualifying event for the Boston marathon that takes place every June.

⇥ Molière in Nova Scotia ⇤

In 1743, the theatre world of Nova Scotia enjoyed a North American first. That year, Paul Macarene, Nova Scotia's commander-in-chief, produced a version of his translation of Molière's *Misanthrope* as part of the Christmas celebrations at Fort Anne. It was the first performance of the great French playwright's work in either French or English in North America.

⇥ New Year's resolution: no more levees! ⇤

On New Year's Day, many Maritimers head out to the levees. At each of the three provincial government houses, the lieutenant-governor now welcomes New Year's guests, but levees were not always popular with the viceregals. From 1816 to 1820, Lord Dalhousie served as Nova Scotia's lieutenant-governor. He was not a fan of levees and wrote the following: "Held a levee as is usual on new year's day. A most ridiculous ceremony and troublesome from the frequency of them." For a number of years, levees were for men only, but that tradition has changed, albeit not always with enthusiasm. As late as 1974, Prince Edward Island's lieutenant-governor, Gordon Bennett, announced that if they desired, Island women could attend the annual New Year's levee at Government House, although he admitted he reached his decision "rather reluctantly."

✢ A kinder, gentler extermination ✦

Ah, the pipes, the pipes. They continue to stir many a Maritime heart. But they sometimes had other uses, as this 1939 account from Andrew Mcphail of Orwell, Prince Edward Island attests: "The mill...was leased by a man named Malcolm Gillis. He played the bagpipes, and wore a scotch bonnet for the ceremonial. He would not play without that emblem. Twice a year he would play his pipes in the dairy to drive away the rats. It was long before we learned that music was a thing to be enjoyed for itself and not for any ulterior purpose. Such as freedom from rats."

✢ The voice of the Canadiens ✦

Born in Whitney Pier, Cape Breton, Danny Gallivan was an avid sportsman who got into sports broadcasting at a local radio station in Antigonish while studying at St. Francis Xavier University, and at Halifax's CJCH radio. He soon became a popular announcer at local hockey games, and his style caught the attention of the folks with the Montreal Canadiens hockey team. He became the voice of *les Canadiens*, and in 1980 was inducted into the Nova Scotia Sports Hall of Fame. His career with the Canadiens lasted from 1952 to 1984. He died in 1993, but will always be remembered as one of hockey's greatest sports announcers.

✦ Howe's home sweet home ✦

World travel can be a wonderful education helping people develop an appreciation of what the world has to offer. But Nova Scotia's nineteenth-century statesman, Joseph Howe, liked his native province best. He once penned these lines as part of his poem "The Blue Nose":

> Let the Frenchman delight in his vine-covered vales,
> Let the Greek toast his old classic ground;
> Here's the land where the bracing Northwester prevails,
> And where jolly Blue Noses abound.

✦ Signatures, sailors, and sighs ✦

Autograph albums were common possessions for most Victorian ladies. I recently came across one assembled by my great-great-aunt Hannah Burns. She kept her album as a girl while living with her family in the lighthouse on Wedge Island, at the mouth of Nova Scotia's St. Mary's River. Her album begins on March 23, 1883. One friend, by the name of Leddie wrote: "While on this lonely isle you stand, and gently view the sea and sand, think of a friend you cannot see, but think that I remember thee." Hannah's friend, Laura Hemloe wrote: "May the hinges of our friendship never rust." Most interesting is this inscription from a writer simply called Your Friend Sailor: "Love is sweet, but oh how bitter, To love a chap and then not get him." Aunt Hannah never married.

✦ Hollywood's connections to Saint John ✦

What do the late actor Walter Pidgeon and movie star Donald Sutherland have in common? Well, aside from looks, talent, and money, they both hail from Saint John, New Brunswick. That town contributed greatly to the Hollywood talent pool. After all, film and studio giant Louis B. Mayer grew up in Saint John. New Brunswick musicians also contributed to movie history when, in May of 1907, they accompanied a silent picture at the Nickle Theatre in Saint John. What's so special about that, you ask? Well, as far as can be determined, they were the first live musicians to accompany a moving picture.

The Saint John Evening Times for May 1, 1907, read: "There are no long waits at the Nickle, but a continuous performance from 12 noon until 6, and from 7 until 10:30 every night...with their usual regard for patrons, the Keith management have provided a ladies' toilet inside the theatre, and before long a regular cloak room will be added to the other accommodations."

CHAPTER FIVE

HARD TIMES IN THE MARITIMES

✦ An ideal job for chocolate lovers ✦

When the French ship *Le Chameau* was wrecked off Louisbourg in 1746, its cargo was so valuable that divers were brought from Quebec to salvage some of its treasure. The only protection these hardy eighteenth-century divers had from the icy waters off Cape Breton was a thick layer of grease and a diet rich in chocolate. Makes me shiver just to think of it!

✦ Good news to the ears of Nova Scotia criminals ✦

March 29, 1841, was a good day for Nova Scotian criminals who were scheduled to receive severe punishment for some crime or another. On that date, an act issued by the Nova Scotia Provincial Parliament in Halifax and signed by the lieutenant-governor, stated that punishment by whipping, using the pillory, or cutting off the ears of offenders was abolished.

Mysterious cargo ✦ aboard the "silk" and ✦ "fish" trains

During World War One, trains from across Canada transported people and supplies for the war effort to Halifax for embarkation to Europe. Two special trains travelled under code names. The outgoing "silk" train carried, not fabric, but Chinese immigrant workers who were shipped overseas to work for the war effort. The special incoming trains designated "fish" trains didn't carry fish, but shipments of gold from Europe to pay for Canadian goods.

✦ Acadian additions to Prince Edward Island ✦

When Halifax was founded in 1749, Nova Scotia's Acadian population could see where British colonization was leading—to a strong fortress against the French and the increased immigration of *les Anglais*. This is in part why in that same year approximately one thousand Acadians moved to Prince Edward Island, then known as Isle St. Jean. These settlers were followed by another five hundred the next year. The exodus continued and by 1776, a year after the Acadian deportation, the Island's Acadian population had reached over four and a half thousand.

✦ (Mount) Hope for those with mental illness ✦

Services and treatment for the mentally ill have seen major changes in Maritime Canada since the nineteenth century. In the 1830s, New Brunswick's cholera hospital was also used as an insane asylum, and by 1847, that province had opened its first asylum devoted to treating those with mental illnesses. That same year, Prince Edward Island opened a combined asylum and poor house, and thirty years later, opened an institution solely dedicated to the treatment of mental illness. In the mid-nineteenth century, American philanthropist Dorothea Dix, travelled the world advocating better treatment for the mentally ill. In 1845, she was invited to Nova Scotia where, upon her recommendations, a hospital for treating the mentally ill was opened in 1859. It was called the Mount Hope Asylum and Hospital for the Insane.

✦ Maritime munitions for World War Two ✦

Robb Engineering Limited was founded by Alexander Robb in Amherst, Nova Scotia. Shortly after the American Civil War, the company began manufacturing stoves—a commodity it had previously imported from the United States. Robb worked to establish a domestic manufacture for iron stoves and other foundry items, and his company eventually went on to manufacture a full range of industrial supplies, including world-renowned industrial engines. During World War Two, Robb's was one of the largest manufacturers of munitions for the British, Canadian, American, and French governments.

⚜ A human fire alarm ⚜

Sirens from fire engines and wails from smoke alarms have become common sounds of warning when a fire breaks out. In the Maritimes of the eighteenth and nineteenth centuries, the cry of "fire" must have certainly rung out numerous times given the number of wooden buildings in most parts of our region. Many communities once hired criers to announce a fire alarm and call out the volunteer fire crews. Well, it seems one fellow kept his job as fire alarm longer than most. As late as 1885, Charlottetown's crier was still being used to publicly announce the fire alarm.

Prior to 1885, citizens of Charlottetown were required to help fight fires, and had to keep emergency firefighting supplies on hand in their homes. If they lived close to one of the town's street lamps, they had the additional daily responsibility of cleaning and lighting that lamp.

⚜ The *Atlantic Advocate* for African Canadians ⚜

Published between 1915 and 1917, the *Atlantic Advocate* was the first periodical devoted to the interests of African Canadians living in the Atlantic provinces. In its inaugural issue, the paper stated its objectives: "The *Atlantic Advocate* aims to show our people the need of unity, the desire to stand always for the right, to keep before them the dignity of true and honest toil; to teach them to keep themselves sober, temperate and honest; to encourage them to march steadily on with a true determination to work, save and endure; always keeping their mind's eye on the great goal of progress."

⤳ A riot caused by *lack* of alcohol? ⤶

Among the many reasons given for the VE Day riots in Halifax on May 7 and 8, 1945, was the severe wartime restriction on the legal consumption of alcohol, even though many prominent citizens lobbied for a more enlightened approach. In a wartime report to the government, folklorist Helen Creighton wrote: "I have yet to meet a travelled person who has a good word to say for our liquor laws, whether they themselves are drinking people or not. By this stupidity, don't you think we are letting our servicemen and women down?"

⤳ The SS *Atlantic* disaster ⤶

Before the *Titanic* disaster in 1912, the wreck of the SS *Atlantic* off Lower Prospect, Nova Scotia, in 1873 was considered the biggest ship disaster in modern history. The SS *Atlantic* was headed out of Liverpool, England, for New York with 811 passengers and a crew of 141 when, on April 1, it met with a severe storm, and its captain decided to steam for Halifax. It struck against the rocky shore, and all the port lifeboats were swept away. Many passengers drowned in their bunks; others died in the surf; some clung to the rigging. All the women perished, and only one child survived.

⤳ An auction of individuals ⤶

During the nineteenth century, destitute people were auctioned off to individuals who would provide for their care in exchange for work. One 1822 account from the Southampton, Nova Scotia, township records notes: "Meeting held at Mr. Henry Furlong's...agreed that this township doth agree to keep one half of Henry G., pauper for life providing that the township of Amherst should agree to keep the other half...during his life; if they do not we shall stand trial."

Another account from the same township records—this time for 1837: "Jeremiah N., pauper put up to auction, to be provided for by Martin

Hoeg for 14 pounds, 15 shillings. Two children (John Edmund R. and Amelia L.) put up for auction. Lowest bidder Andrew Herrett for one shilling and ten pence per week."

☀ Death for desertion ☀

In 1807, crew members of the British frigate *Leopard* boarded the American vessel *Chesapeake* and removed several men they claimed were deserters from the British navy. The men were brought to Halifax, tried as deserters, and two of the unfortunates were flogged to death on the waterfront.

☀ A celebrated naval battle ☀

The battle between the American navy's USS *Chesapeake* and the British frigate HMS *Shannon* during the War of 1812 is legendary. Celebrated in story and folk song is the tale of the British winning the naval battle between the two ships outside Boston Harbour, and the victorious *Shannon* bringing the defeated *Chesapeake* into Halifax Harbour to great acclaim. Yet, the battle itself is most remembered for the dying words of the American captain James Lawrence who, though mortally wounded, extolled his crew: "Tell the men to fire faster. Fight 'til she sinks, boys. Don't give up the ship."

☀ Benefits for "the gentler sex" ☀

Being a member of what used to be condescendingly known as "the gentler sex" had its advantages for at least one woman in colonial Prince Edward Island. Eighteenth-century punishments for what we would consider minor infractions today were often harsh and extreme. On February 19, 1778, a servant named Elizabeth Mutely was convicted of robbing her master of a sum just over seven pounds. Her punishment of death by hanging was the first death sentence pronounced in the new colony. However, Elizabeth was not the first person executed on the Island—because of her gender, no man would come forward to act as executioner. Elizabeth Mutely was pardoned.

✦ Moncton's great Intercolonial Railway fire ✦

On the evening of February 24, 1906, a fire broke out in the Intercolonial Railway paint shop in Moncton. It raged for three hours. The destruction covered over two and a half hectares and the cost of the damages was said to exceed one million dollars. Miraculously, only one man, Abram Jones, lost his life when he returned to the paint shop to retrieve the cash box.

✦ The saltwater cure for seasickness ✦

In 1775, Thomas Curtis left London, England, to come to St. John's Island (now Prince Edward Island). He was eager to experience new adventures. Unfortunately, this meant crossing the ocean and being seasick. Thomas decided to take a common cure of the day—drinking sea water. He wrote: "I found it to be a good phisick [sic]. Several mornings I drank half a pint and found it a Suitable Quality…Others drank more. I have seen some of the men drink a Quart. Then it always operated powerfully upwards and downwards." Thomas's passage cost twenty pounds, and being a young man of some means, he was able to bring along more fine provisions than most for the sea voyage. These included four dozen white shirts, six assorted firearms, and several hundred pounds of powder. For himself and his manservant, Thomas also brought two barrels of beef, two barrels of flour and—this will tell you what his priorities were—a hundred bottles of porter, cider, and rum.

✦ A welcome stay at the station ✦

In the Victorian era, and into the first two decades of the twentieth century, homeless men could often find temporary shelter in the local police stations of the Maritimes. In some cases, homeless men were accommodated for the duration of the cold winter months. This didn't always please the authorities or public-minded citizens. When police gave shelter to an infirm pauper in 1879, the *Charlottetown Examiner* chastised the local constabulary for operating what it called The City Hospital. The practice of providing temporary shelter to indigent people lasted for several decades. The Charlottetown city marshal's report for the month of December 1913, listed among his duties: impounding cows and horses, responding to sixteen robberies, and caring for twelve "men seeking lodgings in Police Station as vagrants."

✣ Struggling to smile ✣

I was born in 1950, and well remember the time when many people in Maritime Canada didn't have the dental hygiene habits they have today. Lack of funds, and more importantly, lack of dentists in many rural areas meant people generally had poor dental hygiene, and some, like a few of my own relatives, had all their teeth removed while still in their teens. An interesting example of a lack of dental hygiene knowledge comes from a report by Prince Edward Island Red Cross nurse Amy MacMahon, who in 1921 conducted a health survey among Island school children. She reported that in some homes there was only one toothbrush for the entire family, and that was used only on Sundays and holidays.

✣ POWs in Amherst? ✣

During World War One, the former Malleable Iron Foundry in Amherst was home to one of Canada's largest prisoner of war camps. In operation from 1915 to 1919, the camp held up to eight hundred internees, most of them German POWs. Despite a riot in 1915, these prisoners remained, for the most part, cooperative and enjoyed many privileges, including participating in social clubs and sports. These activities included fencing matches and musical reviews.

⇥ Nova Scotia's most famous POW ⇤

One of the men incarcerated at the Amherst POW camp in 1917 was famed Russian revolutionary Leon Trotsky. En route from New York to Russia, his ship made a stopover in Halifax where he was taken off, and held for a short time at Citadel Hill. He was then transferred to Amherst where he was held for four months.

In Trotsky's 1930 autobiography, *My Life*, he writes: "The police left my wife and children in Halifax; the rest of us were taken by train to Amherst, Nova Scotia, a camp for German prisoners. And there, in the office, we were put through an examination the like of which I had never before experienced, even in the Peter and Paul fortress. For in the Czar's fortress the police stripped me and searched me in privacy, whereas here our democratic allies subjected us to this shameful humiliation before a dozen men. I can remember Sergeant Olsen, a Swedish-Canadian with a red head of the criminal-police type, who was the leader of the search. The *canaille* [riff-raff] who had arranged all this from a distance knew well enough that we were irreproachable Russian revolutionaries returning to our country, liberated by the revolution."

⇥ World news at Joggins' Wonderland Theatre ⇤

In the early morning of April 15, 1912, nineteen-year-old Edmund Burke was up in his Joggins, Nova Scotia, home listening to his wireless radio receiver. He was picking up regular shipping broadcasts from Cape Cod when he was stunned to hear the radio messages from the *Carpathia* as it steamed to rescue survivors from the famed unsinkable *Titanic*. Later that morning, Edmund posted the news on a blackboard in the window of his father's Wonderland Theatre, but the locals didn't believe it and thought Edmund was joking; however, the morning papers confirmed his statements.

✦ A spy among the ranks ✦

Eighteenth-century French soldier Thomas Pichon served at Louisbourg, and later at Fort Beauséjour in what would become New Brunswick. He penned a book about his experiences that is a valuable resource for scholars of eighteenth-century colonial life. However, that is not the work for which he is best remembered—it seems that Thomas Pichon was also a spy and a cad who preyed upon young women. While working for the French as a secretary, he supplied valuable information to the English. When Fort Beauséjour fell to the English, Pichon worked as a spy in Halifax and later in London, England, under the name Tyrell. He died in 1781, a broken man with a sullied reputation.

✦ Literally dodging the bullet ✦

On May 6, 1937, the great German airship *Hindenburg* burst into flames while trying to dock at Lakehurst, New Jersey. But you may not know that during an earlier flight, it almost didn't make it past Nova Scotia. On its first transatlantic voyage of that year, as the *Hindenburg* passed over Cape Breton, it appeared to many of the spectators that the huge dirigible would hit the Grand Narrows Bridge. "Big Gordie" Macneil, a veteran of World War One, was all for shooting it down to save the bridge. Luckily, his colonel, Willie G. Macrea, was visiting from Baddeck and intervened before there was a disaster. The *Hindenburg* sailed blissfully on, unaware of the fate it would later encounter.

✦ First Nations' fight to enlist ✦

First Nations' war veterans of the Maritime provinces served Canada with valour and dedication. Over 150 Mi'kmaq men signed up during World War One, and over 250 Mi'kmaq enlisted in World War Two. Although they could fight alongside other troops, in order for Mi'kmaq to enlist in World War Two, they had to give up their Indian status. During the first three years of the war, the Canadian Air Force had a rule that only recruits of "pure European descent" would be accepted. The navy required each applicant to "be a British born subject, of a White Race." The Army and Merchant Marines didn't have such restrictions in World War Two. Later, over sixty Mi'kmaq enlisted for service in the Korean War.

⤏ Leaving for greener pastures ⤎

The "brain drain" of Maritime talent has been going on for centuries. The worst decade in the twentieth century was the 1920s. It is estimated that 147,000 people left the Maritimes for the greener pastures of Upper Canada or the northeastern United States, even before the Great Depression, known as the Hungry Thirties. Some areas were decimated. For example, in a ten-year period the population of Amherst, Nova Scotia, fell by 25 percent.

⤏ Sight saving in Halifax ⤎

Hundreds of adults and children were left blind, or had their sight severely damaged during the Halifax Explosion. In Halifax, a school known as the Special Class for Sight Saving was established for children at the Tower Road School. The injured children worked in an especially bright classroom, and most of their school work was done orally since few could see well enough to read and write. Even homework was curtailed as many children not only had poor sight, but also poor lighting at their homes and temporary shelters.

⤏ The story of Country Harbour ⤎

Country Harbour, on Nova Scotia's east coast, is currently experiencing a growth as a result of natural gas production from the offshore gas fields. It looks as if its time has finally come. This beautiful harbour has long rivalled Halifax Harbour, and during the nineteenth century, it vied to be the terminus of the Intercolonial Railway. And here's an interesting bit of World War Two trivia. When things looked bad for the Allies, the British, and Canadian governments considered moving the entire Royal Navy to Country Harbour for safety. After all, it was huge, mainly ice free, and relatively unknown.

☞ Benedict Arnold's escape from New Brunswick ☜

Ask any American child the name of one of that country's most infamous traitors, and Benedict Arnold will be a common answer. But Mr. Arnold also made a bad reputation for himself in New Brunswick. He arrived in Saint John from England in 1785, and planned to enter the commercial trade with the West Indies. However, with his reputation as an American traitor and his arrogant manner, he proved unpopular in his new home as well. He fought with his business partners and his effigy was even burned in the street. He left Canada in disgrace, and wrote of Saint John as "a shipwreck from which I have escaped."

☞ Sharks in Halifax Harbour ☜

You bet. And sometimes they can be dangerous. In a collection of oral histories, Stan Purdy told author Joe Brown that once, probably in the 1940s, a huge shark charged his sister while she was swimming off Devil's Island, a small island at the mouth of Halifax harbour. Men from the island found the shark and speared it, but the animal escaped. What they believed was the same shark was found dead a few days later at nearby Herring Cove. When cut open, the head of a man was found inside.

☞ Winnie's view of Halifax ☜

During World War Two, Halifax's contributions to the war efforts were not always recognized—partially because of secrecy and partially because of ignorance. However, on September 14, 1943, Winston Churchill paid an unexpected visit to Halifax. He toured the city, and surprised citizens who were shocked to see the great "Winnie" on our side of the pond. After viewing the city, and its civilian and military defenses, Sir Winston remarked to Halifax's Mayor Lloyd, "Now, sir, we know your city is something more than a shed on a wharf."

☞ Love and marriage (and citizenship) ☜

The year was 1946. Annette Landry of Cape Breton married George Ling of Prince Edward Island. In those days marriage between a Chinese man and a non-Chinese woman was rare in Canada, and Annette was dismayed to learn from officials that, as a result of her marriage to Ling, she would have to forfeit her Canadian citizenship. She fought the directive and kept her citizenship, partly because the Canadian government finally allowed Chinese immigrants, like her husband George, to attain Canadian citizenship in 1947.

☞ Quarantined on Partridge Island ☜

Used as a quarantine station since 1785, Partridge Island in Saint John Harbour has seen many arrivals isolated to protect the town and region from infectious disease. Its busiest time occurred in 1847, when sixteen thousand Irish immigrants escaping the Potato Famine arrived at Saint John. During its tenure as a quarantine station, over two thousand immigrants and health care workers perished on Partridge Island. A Celtic cross was erected on the Island in 1927, and in 1974, Partridge Island was declared a National Historic Site.

☞ A holiday gift from New Brunswick to Boston ☜

A giant Nova Scotia Christmas tree is lighted before an outdoor audience of thousands in Boston every year. It is donated as a gift to the people of Boston for their help after the 1917 Halifax Explosion. At one time, New Brunswick sent a similar gift to Boston. That Christmas tree was given by the children of New Brunswick to the children of Boston as a remembrance of the time when Boston's citizens sent aid to Saint John after that city was devastated by a fire in 1877. The fire, which took place on a day known as Black Wednesday, left 13,000 people in Saint John homeless. Beginning in 1988, the New Brunswick tree was sent annually for ten years, but the tradition was discontinued in 1998.

⟶ Canada's oldest-standing courthouse ⟵

Built in 1805, the Argyle Township Court House and Gaol at Tusket, Nova Scotia is Canada's oldest-standing courthouse. The building had jail cells on the lower floor and a courthouse on the second story. The region's Supreme Court sat in the courthouse for the last time in 1925, and the jail closed shortly after. The courthouse was used until 1976. After several years of abandonment the building was converted into a museum that opened in 1983. It houses the regional genealogical society's records, and provides a hearty welcome to one and all.

⟶ Halifax, Canada's Confederate headquarters ⟵

Many Nova Scotians were very involved in the American Civil War. For instance, famed statesman Joseph Howe's son, Frederick, fought and was injured for the Union cause. The *Halifax Sun* called the city "a hot southern town" due to the number of Confederate sympathizers and merchants smuggling arms to the southern forces. In fact, the Confederate's informal headquarters was housed at the Waverley Hotel, which is still in operation on Barrington Street.

⟶ An African Canadian earns his wings ⟵

After he graduated from Dartmouth High School, Allan Bundy enlisted in the Royal Canadian Air Force to serve in World War Two. While other young Dartmouth men had preceded Allan, he was the first African Canadian to earn his wings and be commissioned in the RCAF. It wasn't as easy as it sounds for Mr. Bundy. In a November 5, 1998, statement before the Standing Senate Committee on Legal and Constitutional

Affairs Calvin Ruck, a Nova Scotia senator reminded members that "when the Royal Canadian Navy came into being in 1910 under the government of Sir Wilfrid Laurier, rules and regulations were put in place. The first regulation with respect to enlistment stated explicitly that all recruits had to be members of the white race. That regulation was in effect until 1943...Another branch of service where there were problems was the Royal Canadian Air Force. There was a gentleman from Dartmouth by the name of Allan Bundy, a high school graduate and a black man. He had seen other school chums go to the RCAF, and he thought it was just a matter of going to the recruiting station. He went to a recruiting station in Halifax on Barrington Street...When he went there, he was refused entry into the RCAF and told to join the army. Again, he pursued the matter....When conscription came into force, the RCMP visited his home because he did not respond to his notice to enlist. He wanted to go into the RCAF, and he felt if he was not good enough for the RCAF, why should he be good enough for the army? He told the RCMP to arrest him because he was prepared to go to jail. Along the line, however, something happened. He received notice to report to a recruiting station and was accepted into the RCAF. "

⤞ Charlottetown's wicked reputation ⤝

As the largest city and busiest port in the Maritimes, Halifax had (during the eighteenth and nineteenth centuries) the dubious honour of being known by visiting sailors as Black Town. If sin was what you were looking for, Halifax was your destination. Rum shops, bordellos, and places where sailors weren't safe from crimps and thugs were common. But the big towns weren't the only ones that had sullied names. When James MacGregor visited Charlottetown in 1791, he reported: "In a few minutes I found Charlottetown to be wicked enough for a larger town. Swearing and drunkenness abounded."

✧ Memorial to Halifax Explosion victims ✧

Halifax Harbour, December 6, 1917. After a collision with the relief ship *Imo*, the supply ship *Mont Blanc*, filled with explosives, disintegrated in a fire ball. Halifax was devastated. It is estimated that over two thousand people were killed. Approximately nine thousand people were injured or disabled. Perhaps no other incident in Maritime history has been so studied and written about. The Halifax Explosion remains one of Canada's greatest disasters. The Halifax Explosion Memorial Bell Tower at Fort Needham Park overlooking the explosion site, was dedicated in 1985 as a permanent memorial to the victims.

✧ A world leader's beginnings in Windsor ✧

During World War One, Jewish people living in the United States formed their own battalion, and before embarking to fight in Europe, they carried out basic training at Fort Edward in Windsor, Nova Scotia. One of those soldiers was David Ben-Gurion, who would go on to become the first prime minister of Israel.

✧ Branded a chicken thief ✧

The Supreme Court of Nova Scotia's first session took place in Halifax on October 29, 1754. One poor soul, a man named John Moor, was convicted of stealing a dozen chickens. His sentence was to have the letter T branded on his thumb to mark him as an offender in case he committed another crime.

✧ Spanish treasure on the Fundy shore ✧

During the War of 1812, the British brig *Plumper* left Halifax carrying seventy thousand pounds in coin as payment for the military fighting the Americans. It went down in a severe December storm. Its resting place was in twenty-three metres of water off Dipper Harbour in the Bay of Fundy. Some of its treasure was recovered, but for a number of years locals were reputed to find Spanish coins washing ashore on the beach. They called these tiny bits of treasure plumpers.

✣ Wartime convoys in Maritime ports ✣

Halifax was the primary North American assembly and debarkation point for the convoys of naval and merchant ships carrying arms and supplies to Europe during the two world wars, but the ports of Sydney and North Sydney in Cape Breton were also major players. The slower convoys left from these two ports, and helped bring much-needed military and relief supplies for the war effort.

✣ Training in penitentiaries ✣

Before the Nova Scotia penitentiary merged with the prison at Dorchester, New Brunswick, in 1880, it was located in Halifax within Point Pleasant Park. Male inmates were taught trades such as tailoring, blacksmithing, shoemaking, and broom manufacturing. Female inmates, segregated from the men, had a small nursery for their children and were trained in spinning, knitting, and caring for the laundry.

✣ Maritime fortune in a time of war ✣

Wars are always sad and difficult, but they usually bring an economic swell for someone, somewhere. The fortunes of the Maritimes rose and fell during times of war. One such example was the increase in the business of supplying masts and other wood for the British Navy. Much of the wood needed to build the huge eighteenth- and early-nineteenth-century Royal Navy ships came from Sweden through the area around the Baltic Sea, but when Napoleon cut off the Baltic supply of lumber, Britain looked to its colonies on the Atlantic seaboard. Nova Scotia and New Brunswick became the primary suppliers of wood products, especially tall, straight pine used for the vast quantities of masts and spars needed for fully rigged ships of war.

✧ Our friends the enemy ✦

On July 28, 2005, the Canadian government offered an official apology to the Acadians in recognition of the British expulsion of its citizens in 1755. Local British troops were aided in this mass deportation by troops from the American colonies. Before this event, many Acadians traded freely with the colonials in New England despite occasional raids into Acadian territory by the New Englanders. This strange relationship of clandestine trade caused the Acadians to refer to their English neighbours to the south as "our friends the enemy."

✧ Rough journeys in desperate times ✦

From the 1890s to the 1930s, large numbers of Maritime men boarded trains to seek work in the wheat fields of the Canadian Prairies. These modes of transport became known as Harvest Trains. But for some of our Maritime travellers, the adventure was less than smooth. The August 12, 1904, edition of the *New Glasgow Eastern Chronicle* said: "It is also hoped that the weird tales from along the route of fighting, stealing, blood, and carnage will be lacking this year."

✧ The end of privateering ✦

We usually think of the days of legalized piracy, known as privateering, as taking place primarily in the eighteenth century. But during the American Civil War, the southern forces issued letters of marque to enable civilian vessels to capture ships friendly to the northern cause. This made things difficult for ships sailing out of Maritime harbours such as Halifax, Saint John, and Yarmouth because American ships from both factions would lay in wait outside these ports to try and capture enemy ships.

✧ Our Lady's Bell ✦

When the Acadians were being deported in 1755, the priest at Doucette's

Point across from Port Royal, instructed the villagers to burn the town. But before the English came to take them away, the people buried the church bell. After many years, some of the Acadians made their way back to Nova Scotia. Matthiew Doucette was past sixty years of age, but he struggled to return to his destroyed village, where he found the buried bell. He gave it to the Acadian community at Baie Sainte Marie over 160 kilometres away, where it was hung in the church, and is reverently known as Our Lady's Bell.

☞ The *Titanic* and the Cape Bear lighthouse ☜

Cape Bear lighthouse, located at the east end of Prince Edward Island near Murray Harbour, was erected in 1881. While its primary function was to act as a beacon to local fishermen, it did double duty as part of a chain of seven wireless stations for the Marconi Wireless Company. The lighthouse, no doubt, helped saved many local ships from disaster, but it was its part in the greatest sea tragedy of the twentieth century that ensured its place in history. Shortly after 11:40 p.m. on April 14, 1912, the people manning the wireless station at Cape Bear lighthouse were the first to hear the distress signal from the *Titanic*, soon after it struck an iceberg off Newfoundland.

☞ No Slave Masters Allowed ☜

Holding and trading in enslaved persons was not uncommon in the early Maritimes. Ads such as the following appeared in the *Halifax Gazette*: "Public Auction: On Monday, 3rd of November 1760—To Be Sold at the house of John Rider, two slaves, viz: boy and girl about eleven years of age; likewise a puncheon of choice old cherry brandy with sundry other articles." After all, slavery wasn't abolished in the British Empire until 1833. The Society of Friends, also known as the Quakers, was one of the earliest groups to voice their support for the abolition of slavery. So it must be assumed that the Quaker community that prospered in

Dartmouth, Nova Scotia, from 1784 until 1792, held no enslaved persons. We do know, however, that the small Quaker community in early Loyalist New Brunswick was so against slavery that they posted a sign outside their village of Beaver Harbour on the Bay of Fundy that read: "No Slave Masters Admitted."

☞ The gift of freedom ☜

Some Christmas gifts are beyond precious. On December 25, 1790, John Burbidge of Cornwallis, Nova Scotia, granted a gift to three of his slaves. He wrote a statement concerning Faney and her children, seventeen-year-old Peter, seven-year-old Hannah, and two-year-old Flora, with the admonition that they be given their freedom, and that "they shall be taught to read…they shall be dismissed with two good sutes [sic] of aparal [sic], one fit for Sundays, one for every day suitable for such servants." The gift of freedom—I can think of none better.

An 1802 census of the Aylesford area in Nova Scotia lists three enslaved persons. Two of these slaves, Cuff and Anthony, were listed as property of the Van Buskirk family. When slavery was abolished in the British colonies in 1833, Anthony was given his freedom and allowed to take the Van Buskirk name. Cuff, who had died before 1833, was symbolically granted his freedom posthumously.

☞ The Dutch Maritimes ☜

The lands of the Acadians have traded hands many times. Treaties between France and Britain saw the territory transferred in several bids to shuffle the lands and its people back and forth between the two super powers, but chances are, few Maritimers know that at one time the land was also held by Dutch forces. In 1674, the Dutch sea captain Jurriaen Aernoutsz, captured the French fortress on the Penobscot River and took the Acadian governor prisoner. He renamed Acadia New Holland, and a New York merchant named Cornelis Steenwyck was given the title governor of the coasts and countries of Nova Scotia and Acadia. However, New Englanders from Boston weren't happy with the situation and took back the lands by force. They didn't stay, and the area reverted back to the French.

✣ Murder in the new colony ✣

Just a few weeks after Halifax was founded in June of 1749, Abraham Goodsides was fatally stabbed by Peter Cartcel. Governor Cornwallis and six of his counsellors acted as judge and jury, and five days after the trial, Peter was hanged. Peter Cartcel earned himself the distinction of being the first man tried and executed for murder in the new colony.

✣ The wrath of the winter sea ✣

It is especially dangerous to be shipwrecked off our Maritime coast in the winter. On January 1, 1824, the barque *Jessie* was wrecked off tiny St. Paul Island—known as the Graveyard of the Gulf. Out of a complement of twenty-six people, eleven managed to reach the shore and climb the steep, icy cliffs of the island. Despite being able to light fires and attract the attention of those on the mainland, the pack ice was so thick and dangerous that a rescue was impossible, and all eleven people perished after having survived the wrath of the sea.

In 1836, Captain Hubert Aucoin of Cheticamp managed to land on St. Paul Island after his fishing smack was destroyed by crushing pack ice. He didn't survive, but did leave this poignant epitaph etched into a rock: "Hubert Aucoin, son of Anselme Aucoin, died of hunger and thirst. If you find my body, bury it."

✣ American prisoners in the Northwest Arm ✣

During the War of 1812, prisoners from the United States were incarcerated on Melville Island in Halifax's Northwest Arm. Benjamin Waterhouse, a surgeon from a captured American privateer, recorded these May 13, 1813, observations: "I had time to notice the occupations of these poor fellows. Some were washing their own clothes; others mending them. Others were intent on ridding their shirts and other clothing from lice which, to the disgrace of the British government, are allowed to infest our prisoners."

Neighbourly
⇥ treatment for Irish ⇤
shipwreck victims

On May 7, 1834, the barque *Astraea*, carrying Irish immigrants from Limerick to Quebec, was wrecked at Lorraine Head, Cape Breton. Only 3 of the 251 passengers survived, and many of the steerage passengers, who had been sleeping, were naked or only in nightclothes when retrieved. Out of respect for the dead, the local inhabitants managed to bury each one with a suit of clothes: shirt, jacket, and trousers for the men, and petticoat and dress for the women. It is also said that they were buried before sunset because of the belief that doing so would prevent their spirits from being doomed to roam the land.

⇥ Lost treasure found ⇤

In July 1725, the French transport ship *Le Chameau* left France en route to Quebec with several military and political dignitaries, and a fortune in gold and silver aboard. Sadly, it went down off Louisbourg at Kelpy Cove, and although the site of the wreck was known, its treasure was not recovered. That is until September of 1965, when treasure diver Alex Storm and his crew found its treasure. It was one of the richest shipwreck finds off the coast of Maritime Canada.

⇥ A train missed, a life saved ⇤

Arthur Lismer was one of Canada's finest artists, and a founding member of the famous Group of Seven. Born in England, Mr. Lismer worked and taught in several Canadian locales, and from 1916 to 1919, served as principal of the Victoria School of Art and Design (precursor of the Nova Scotia College of Art and Design). Although he lived in Bedford, he commuted by train to Halifax. On the morning of December 6, 1917, Arthur missed his morning train. That missed train ride probably saved his life—on the very morning he was late, the great Halifax Explosion destroyed the part of the city he would have travelled through.

⇥ A life-saving decision ⇤

Audrey Middleton, a dear friend, recently told me this remarkable story. Early in December of 1917, Audrey and her family were living near Kentville, Nova Scotia, and her mother was close to her time to deliver Audrey's brother. The family's doctor had travelled to Halifax to attend a conference. However, on December 5, the doctor left the conference and caught the train back to Kentville so he could be with his patient when the baby arrived. Sure enough, the next morning very shortly after nine o'clock, Audrey's brother was born—at almost the exact time of the Halifax Explosion. If the doctor had stayed in Halifax and not come home early to deliver the baby, he would have perished along with others staying at his hotel, which was destroyed. Until the day he died, the doctor claimed that baby saved his life!

⇥ Rebuilding Acadia ⇤

After the expulsion of the Acadians in 1755, it took nine years before the British Lords of Trade informed Lieutenant-Governor Wilmot that the exiles were to be allowed back to the land of their ancestors. In 1764, provided they swore an oath of allegiance to the Crown, exiled Acadians began to make their way back to their traditional homeland. In 1772, several Acadian families from New England settled in the Memramcook Valley. These Acadians began rebuilding their lives on traditional Acadian marshland and attempted to resume life as it had gone on before, which included establishing the first religious parish in Acadia after the deportation. This region is known as the Birthplace of New Acadia.

→ Saint John's Great Conflagration ←

On the evening of January 14, 1837, the city of Saint John experienced one of the worst fires in the history of the Maritimes. Local residents knew the disaster as the Great Conflagration. The glow from the flames could be seen as far away as Fredericton. Burning debris was sent flying over fourteen and a half kilometres away and fully one-third of the commercial district of the city was destroyed.

→ A motivational keg of beer ←

The early colonial governments of our region had small forces of regular military personnel to enforce laws and keep the peace, as well as to serve as first-line defence in case of attack. Still, a larger supplementary force was needed, and the governments imposed a rule of forming local militias. Every small town had them—they were made up of men and boys who were given rudimentary training. Attendance at these militia training sessions was mandatory, but this was not easy to enforce. However, the folks on Prince Edward Island had a grand idea. The first Militia Act for Prince Edward Island, enacted in 1780, called for all males between the ages of sixteen and sixty to bear arms and muster for training one day a year. Apparently, most of the fellows called upon attended. There was the offer of a free keg of beer.

CHAPTER SIX

BY LAND, SEA, AND AIR

The fastest ship in the world!

That was the title earned by the New Brunswick vessel *Marco Polo* after it broke speed records sailing between Australia and England. Built in Saint John in 1851, it was the largest immigrant packet in the world. Packet ships, named for their delivery of mail, were used to carry British royal mail to the colonies and to transport immigrants. *Marco Polo* eventually worked for the famous Blackball Line out of Liverpool, England, but its career ended in 1883, when it was wrecked off Cavendish Beach, Prince Edward Island.

A road trip—without a motor

In 1927, Frank Elliot and George Scott from Amherst, Nova Scotia, travelled across Canada in a Model T Ford. Not an unusual feat, except for one thing—the car had no motor. The buddies advertised their trip from Halifax to Vancouver as the longest tow in the world. Dressed in oilskins and sou'westers, Frank and George equipped their car with a tow bar, and over the duration of their journey, 168 travellers vied for the fun and novelty of hauling them along.

A daredevil flies over Halifax

For ten days in September of 1912, American pilot Charles Walsh flew exhibition flights over Halifax during the Nova Scotia Exhibition. He is believed to be the first person to take off from Halifax, and the first person to fly over that city. But he almost didn't survive the exhibition. He had several accidents, including narrowly missing a cow barn, skimming telegraph wires and a stationary locomotive and, finally, smashing into a board fence and destroying one of his planes. The accidents in Halifax should have been his warning. Thirteen days later, Charles Walsh died in an airplane accident in New Jersey.

◈ Buses overflowing with servicemen and women ◈

My father remembers making the bus trip from Halifax to Sherbrooke along Nova Scotia's eastern shore during World War Two, at a time when hundreds of servicemen and women were trying to travel on the small buses. He told me that the bus would be so full when it left its depot at the Lord Nelson Hotel that it would have to be followed by a number of taxis carrying the overflow. These cabs would discharge their passengers and return to the city as space became available on the bus.

◈ License plates for early automobiles ◈

The first automobile license plates in Canada were issued in Ontario in 1903. Owners were given a patent leather plaque with aluminum numbers. New Brunswick began issuing plates in 1911, and Nova Scotia did the same in 1918, the same year plates were offered to residents of Prince Edward Island. For a number of years previous, Islanders had been issued a number that had to be attached to a plate they made themselves.

◈ An easier commute ◈

Today, making the connection between Nova Scotia and Newfoundland by car is as easy as driving onto the ferry at North Sydney. But it wasn't until 1955 that you could actually drive your vehicle on board. The MV *William Carson* was the first ferry to offer drive-on service. Before that, people wanting to bring their car along to Newfoundland had to have it hoisted aboard and stored with the cargo.

◈ The first flight from the mainland ◈

Air freight and passengers arrive daily on Prince Edward Island, but it is less that one hundred years since the first such arrival took place. The first flight to Prince Edward Island was made on September 25, 1919, by Captain L. E. D Stevens of Truro, Nova Scotia and Lieutenant J. M. Stevenson of Charlottetown. They left Truro in a Curtis airplane and arrived in Charlottetown in slightly over an hour.

⤞ The Island's first airport ⤝

Prince Edward Island's first airport was established on the horse farm of Dr. Jack Jenkins and his wife Louise in the village of Upton. In the early 1920s, the good doctor and his wife took flying lessons, purchased a red de Havilland Puss Moth Airplane, and began regular flights from what became known as Upton Fields—the Island's first airport.

⤞ Canada officially joins Cape Breton ⤝

On August 13, 1955, on one of the hottest days of the summer, one hundred pipers and drummers heralded a procession of dignitaries and citizens to make the first official crossing on the Canso Causeway. For decades there had been talk of making a permanent connection between mainland Nova Scotia and Cape Breton. There were plans for a tunnel and several ideas for bridges, but it wasn't until 1952 that a twenty-three million dollar project for a solid causeway with a swing bridge began. Almost ten million metric tonnes of rock were taken from Cape Porcupine, and the permanent connection was made in December of 1955. But the official party and celebrations were held on August 13. That's the day Cape Bretoners like to say Canada joined the Island. We're glad we did.

⤞ Frozen ferries get dynamic rescue ⤝

The ice packs in the Northumberland Strait can sometimes be overwhelming to ships. Such was the case in 1903 when the January ice pack surrounded the ferry *Stanley* as it tried to make its way between Prince

Edward Island and Nova Scotia. Twenty-seven days later, a rescue attempt was made by the ferry *Minto*. The ice entrapped it too. The passengers from both ferries had to be removed and taken by small iceboats to Pictou. After being stranded for sixty-six days, dynamite was used to free both vessels and the *Stanley* towed the *Minto* back to Pictou.

⤳ Boats for the ice ⤶

Iceboats were once the only method of getting to Prince Edward Island after the winter ice flows set into the Northumberland Strait. These rowboats had iron strips running on the side of the keel. Crew members would row the boats where possible, and when ice made it impossible to continue, would get out and haul the boat, its passengers, and its cargo over the flow. Passengers could reduce their fare if they got out and helped with the work. Ice boats were the primary mode of winter transportation during the nineteenth century, and were used until April of 1917, when the last official ice boat made the crossing and vanished into Maritime history.

⤳ Putting horses out of work ⤶

From the *Halifax Daily Echo*, September 11, 1899, comes this notice: "The first automobile ever seen in Nova Scotia, arrived on the Allan liner *Siberian* from Liverpool [England] this morning. It is a gasoline horseless carriage, owned by William Exshaw, son-in-law of Sir Sanford Fleming. It was built in France and has been run by Mr. Exshaw since the first of the year. The propelling motor is operated by gasoline. The automobile is boxed up, but Mr. Exshaw expects to be driving it around the streets in a few days."

What's yellow
⟿ and green, and beloved ⟻
by many Maritimers?

One of the most recognizable traditional Maritime boats was the dory. The most common colour was yellow, presumably so one could be found in the fog. The dory was the workhorse of the schooner, usually manned by two fellows who became dory mates and learned to work as a finely honed team. Dories could be used for two forms of fishing—handlining, where individual lines with multiple hooks were used to catch fish, or for longlining, where long measures of trawl were played out and later hauled aboard to retrieve the catch. Both forms of fishing are from another age, but dories remain popular pleasure boats along Maritime shores.

⟿ Opposition to the opposite side of the road ⟻

Until April 15, 1923, automobiles, bicycles, and animal-hauled conveyances in Nova Scotia drove on the left side of the road, as they still do in Britain today. But from that day on, all traffic in the province kept to the right. It wasn't a popular change and caused hardships for many. Tram cars in Halifax had to rework their doors so they could open on the opposite side and there were costs involved in changing the track switches. To confuse matters, motorists travelling to New Brunswick had to go back to the left side of the road once they crossed the provincial border. In Nova Scotia's Lunenburg County, 1923 became known as The Year of Free Beef. Teams of oxen had been trained to keep to the left of the road, and some of the poor beasts who couldn't be taught to keep to the right side ended up on the dinner table.

⟿ Coast-to-coast journeys ⟻

Even with the speed of today's jetliners, a flight across Canada is still a long journey. Folks may complain about catching the red-eye, and the long, five-hour flight from Vancouver to Halifax. But that would have been a welcome time for the crew who made the first trans-Canadian flight between the two cities. On October 7, 1920, two flight crews in two airplanes, took eleven days to complete that inaugural flight from coast-to-coast.

It still takes days to drive from one coast of Canada to the other. Imagine how difficult it was for Dr. P. E. Doolittle of the newly formed Canadian Automobile Company, and Edward Flickenger from Ford Motor Company, when they took off on a motor trip across Canada in 1925. The trip from Halifax to Vancouver lasted thirty-nine days, and their Model T Ford had to be carried by rail where roads were unavailable.

⇒ North Sydney, a bustling seaport? ⇐

When the world's shipping enterprises changed from sail power to steam, the effect on the seaport of North Sydney, Nova Scotia, was dramatic. Beginning in the 1850s, vessels from the British, French, and American navies all stopped at North Sydney to refuel with coal. The trade was so brisk that by 1875, North Sydney ranked only behind Halifax, Quebec City, and Montreal in terms of tonnage handled in a Canadian port.

⇒ The *Silver Dart* ⇐

The first powered flight in the British Empire took place on February 23, 1909, when John McCurdy flew the *Silver Dart* for a short distance over the frozen Bras d' Or Lakes at Baddeck. Few Canadians know the fate of that historic airplane. Later that summer, in a display for the military to help raise development funds, the *Silver Dart* landed on the parade ground in Petawawa, Ontario, and was destroyed.

⇒ A link to the mainland ⇐

Today, travel between New Brunswick and Prince Edward Island is easy. Before it was possible to drive between the two provinces, the famous Island ferries carried passengers, freight, and even rail cars back and forth between the Island and New Brunswick or Nova Scotia. Over the years, a number of proposals were made to link the Island with the rest of Canada. These included a pontoon bridge, and various designs for a tunnel. In the 1870s, charismatic Island politician George Howlan suggested a combination tunnel/railway that would run under the water—a method he called a subway. Since 1997, the Confederation Bridge has linked Prince Edward Island to the Mainland.

☌ Canada and Newfoundland united ☌

Even before Newfoundland joined Confederation in 1949, the first of July held special significance for the island colony. For, it was July 1, 1898, that the SS *Bruce* sailed into Sydney Harbour, Nova Scotia, on its inaugural voyage from Port aux Basques, Newfoundland, uniting the Dominions of Canada and Newfoundland by a regular passenger and freight ferry.

☌ Travel takes its toll ☌

Toll highways in Nova Scotia and New Brunswick seem to be here to stay. The Cobequid Pass toll road in Nova Scotia opened in 1997, and New Brunswick opened a section of toll road in 2002. Prince Edward Island doesn't let people away from paying for surface travel either. Drivers have to pay a toll to leave the Island by the fixed link. Some folks heartily agree with this toll system; others are just as opposed.

It seems some of our ancestors didn't take kindly to the idea of toll roads. For example, in 1782, the Government of Nova Scotia began charging tolls on the Old Windsor Road as a means of paying for road improvements. Two toll gates were erected. The one near the Sackville Bridge was destroyed by local inhabitants. Four years later, local farmers were given an exemption from paying the toll, and in 1787, the toll scheme was abandoned. The people had spoken!

⤳ Train tickets for horses ⤶

In the 1850s, the Nova Scotia Railway Company introduced a method of transportation that I find very amusing. In an effort to promote train use to rural farmers, the company offered fares that included the transportation of the farmer's wagon and horse. Eventually, the operators of stagecoaches saw the advantage of this system and loaded the coaches, their horses, and their passengers on the train. Folks with horses saved on horseshoe wear, and the animals arrived rested; however, the train company lost so much on this scheme that they eventually stopped the practice.

⤳ Drinking and driving in the nineteenth century ⤶

The following notice that appeared in the *New Glasgow Enterprise*, October 20, 1888, may describe the first occurrence of drunk driving in Nova Scotia: "A drunken man from Stellarton was gailed [sic] on Sunday [14 October] for disorderly driving on the streets of New Glasgow."

⤳ The years of two fiddles and no plows ⤶

Prince Edward Island's shipbuilding heydays were in the 1850s when Island shipwrights were launching an average of one hundred ships a year—more per capita than any other place in the British Empire. So many workers left the fields for the relative prosperity of the shipbuilding trade that this time of plenty became known as "the years of two fiddles and no plows."

The first steamboat constructed in Canada was named the *Sir Charles Ogle*. That vessel became the first steam ferry in Canada when it was launched in Halifax Harbour on January 1, 1830.

⤳ Wobbly new cyclists hit the road ⤶

In the late 1950s, my grandfather Ernest MacKay used to refer to my bicycle as a wheel. He'd say, "Be careful, and don't fall off your wheel!"

It was a common term for many people back then, one left over from Victorian times. Wheels or bicycles became a huge fad in the 1880s and 1890s, but one not popular with everyone. Take, for example, this notice in the June 5, 1897, *Truro Daily News*: "Some of the antics of the new bicycle riders are very amusing. They want all the road and sometimes both ditches. They are getting past the wobbly stage now and it is quite safe for people to walk along the roads." Or how about the following notice from the 1885 *Charlottetown Patriot*? "Mr Moore collided with a cow, which injured the fork of his wheel and impeded his speed afterwards."

❖ Buckling up in the Maritimes ❖

"Buckle up and save lives" is a phrase familiar to everyone in Canada. Wearing a seat belt while operating a motor vehicle is mandatory in all provinces, but not everyone took to the laws with equal fervour. Ontario and Quebec led the way in 1976. New Brunswick came on board in 1983, Nova Scotia in 1985, and Prince Edward Island waited until 1988.

❖ A long, long walk to Vancouver ❖

Billing themselves the Transcontinental Pedestrians, three Cape Breton men took the challenge offered by a North Sydney businessman, and in 1906, began a foot trek across Canada. They were hoping to win a twelve hundred dollar prize. G. W. Cummings and John MacDonald dropped out in Montreal, but John Hugh Gillis continued on to Vancouver, arriving seven months later to claim his money.

❖ Tangled up on the tracks ❖

The early days of train travel in the Maritimes may sound romantic, but consider how primitive many of these trains were—not to mention the condition of the tracks and rail beds. In his book, *Bay of Chaleur: Forgotten Treasures*, author A. J. McCarthy tells of the 1886 Caraquet and

Gulf Shore Railway Company's route along which trains were actually slowed down because the cars had to push through alders growing by the sides of the tracks.

⇢ Brushing the ice ⇠

Winter travel in the Maritimes was a far more difficult task in our ancestors' time. Rivers and inlets were regularly used as roads once the heavy winter ice set in, but often these transportation routes had their own inherent dangers. In a snowstorm, travellers sometimes got lost or inadvertently followed a frozen river out to the sea or into the channel, and fell through the thin ice. One safeguard against this was the custom of brushing the ice. On the frozen rivers of Prince Edward Island, this was done by placing small spruce trees in holes in the ice about thirty metres apart from one shore to the other. This formed a brush fence and prevented the traveller from venturing out onto dangerous ice.

⇢ New Brunswick's famous Bricklin ⇠

New Brunswick entered the automobile manufacturing world in 1974 when the provincial government helped sponsor the production of a flamboyant, sleek, high-tech car called the Bricklin. Named for the Florida promoter who negotiated the deal with premier Richard Hatfield, the car was reasonably priced and nice-looking, but critics complained that it didn't work all that well. Only 2,880 Bricklins were made—they are collector's items today, but were a political bone of contention in their time.

⇢ A trying trip during the reign of mud ⇠

A trip from Truro to Amherst is but a short journey today. Not so in 1867, according to an account from Dr. D. A. Steele: "In late November ... Archibald and Purdy's stagecoach picked us up at Truro at 11:00 a.m. Three passengers were on board bound to Amherst. There had been a few day's sleighing but now it was the 'reign of mud.' We plodded along through snow, Folly and Great Village and by nightfall had made Purdy's Inn at Westchester. Then, slowly, steadily, we descended and reached Amherst via Morse Corner at 2:00 a.m. having made the trip in fifteen hours."

⇥ PEI's shaky introduction to the automobile ⇤

Automobiles have been travelling on the roads of Prince Edward Island for over a century. Just think back to the long lineups to get your car on a ferry, and you'll realize that throughout most of its history, cars had to be transported to the Island by means other than a fixed link. The first record of an automobile on the Island goes back to 1866, when Father George A. Belcourt, parish priest at Rustico, shipped home an ordinary horse buggy that had been outfitted with a small steam engine to drive the wheels. Once on the Island it was time for a test drive. So, on St. Baptiste Day, June 24 in 1867, Father Belcourt took off in his auto. He went forward and promptly ran off the road. PEI's first car and its first car accident.

⇥ A soft place to land ⇤

In 1936, Charlottetown native, Carl Burke started a small flight route with Canadian Airways Limited making the trip between Moncton and Summerside. Winter travel was very different then. One woman, desperate to get home for her mother's funeral, was offered a unique flight; she later reported: "He asked if I would be willing to jump ten or twelve feet. He didn't dare let the pontoons touch as he might not be able to get into the air again. I said I'd try, so they threw my suitcase out and he said 'Now jump, and good luck.' I prayed to the Lord and made a safe landing. The snow was soft."

CHAPTER SEVEN

MAKING A LIVING

→ High and dry ←

The first dry dock in Canada, and maybe even North America, was used by early French settlers at Chignecto, near where the La Coupe and Aulac Rivers meet in present-day New Brunswick. Vessels could be floated up the river and rested on waters that produced tides up to seven metres high. A system of gates would allow the water to leave with the tide, and block its path back when the tide rose again, leaving the vessel high and dry and ready for repair. After the necessary repairs were made, the gates were opened at high tide, and the vessel could float back down the river. It is believed this dry-docking system was first used around 1690, which would make it Canada's oldest known dry dock.

→ A whale of a tale ←

My sister's late father-in-law, James "Tannie" Kaiser, had some amazing experiences as a young man fishing out of Port Bickerton, Nova Scotia. In 1937, Tannie said their vessel "fetched up solid" many kilometres from shore. They had been lifted up by a whale! "When I looked over the side," Tannie said, "there was whale to port and starboard...it must have weighed 20 to 30 tons."

→ The Antigonish Movement ←

Born in Margaree Forks, Cape Breton, in 1882, Moses M. Coady was inducted into the priesthood in Rome in 1910. Upon his return to Nova Scotia, he began teaching at St. Francis Xavier University. He embraced the concept of lifelong learning, and the belief that fairness and equity in one's work can be realized through co-operatives and community development. Coady's theories, known as the Antigonish Movement, helped make him one of Nova Scotia's most influential educators. In 1959, St. F. X. established the Coady International Institute to help train leaders from around the world in the principles and practices of a people-based approach to development.

⤳ Minto mining ⤶

Although most Canadians think of Cape Breton and Pictou County in Nova Scotia when they think of early coal mining in the Maritimes, the small community of Minto, New Brunswick, can lay claim to being the first east coast region where coal was extracted for commercial use. Famed English diarist Samuel Pepys makes reference to the site in his 1667 diary. That first foray into coal mining was conducted by Charles La Tour in 1643 at Grand Lake, near present-day Minto. The coal was extracted from a small open pit, and shipped to Boston. A monument at Minto marks the site of the first known place for coal mining in North America.

The Joggins area of Nova Scotia was one of the first locales in the Maritimes where coal was mined for export. Joggins coal was offered for sale in Boston as early as 1720, and the ship's log of Captain Hale from Salem, Massachusetts, recounts observations of coal extraction from the Joggins cliffs in 1730. The first official mine opened in 1847.

In Samuel Pepys's diary entry for September 8, 1667, he comments on complaints his boss, Sir George Downing, has made about valuable lands and resources being exchanged to pay government debt and to further treaty negotiations: "He says that this is a piece of shame that never any nation committed, and that our very Lords here of the Council, when he related this matter to them, did not remember that they had agreed to this article; and swears that all their articles are alike, as the giving away Polleroon, and Surinam, and Nova Scotia, which hath a river 300 miles up the country, with copper mines more than Swedeland,

and Newcastle coals, the only place in America that hath coals that we know of; and that Cromwell did value those places, and would for ever have made much of them; but we have given them away for nothing, besides a debt to the King of Denmarke."

✦ A 1695 sawmill? ✦

The lumber industry is New Brunswick's largest commercial enterprise. While several huge factories and mills now process the province's timber, the region was once dotted with hundreds of small sawmills that used the abundant water power from the area's many rivers. The Acadian census of 1695 shows that a seigneur at Nashwaak named Sieur de Chaffours owned a large tract of land on which he had erected a house. He is also reported to have built a sawmill that he operated with his brother. The census is believed to be the first record of a sawmill in New Brunswick.

✦ Strange setting for school ✦

Some kids boast of going to a one-room school but few children today could say they went to school in a tavern. The first known school in Charlottetown was established in 1778. That was the year schoolmaster Alexander Robertson purchased land on the corner of Dorchester and Queen streets and erected the Cross Keys Inn. It may have been a tavern, but Mr. Robertson used one room in his new building to start a private school for those children whose parents could afford the tuition.

✦ Extra! Read all about it! ✦

The Maritimes is a region of newspaper-lovers. In fact, Canada's first paper, the *Halifax Gazette* was published in 1752. New Brunswick's first newspaper, the *Royal Saint John Gazette and Nova Scotia Intelligencer*, began publication in 1783. Prince Edward Island's first newspaper, the *Royal American Gazette and Weekly Intelligencer of the Island of Saint John* began publishing in Charlottetown in 1787. The first French-language newspaper in the Maritimes was *Le Moniteur Acadien*, founded by Israel J. D. Landry in 1867 in Shediac.

The first issue of the *Royal American Gazette and Weekly Intelligencer of The Island of Saint John* was printed on September 15, 1787, by James Robertson. Like many colonial papers of the day, its main focus was on British news and excerpts from other papers. It did try to serve the Loyalists who were settling on St. John's Island during this period by including information about Loyalist land claims, the news from the House of Assembly and official proclamations. The paper, in its original form, did not survive for long—only about a year. The last issue on record was published in 1788.

⇥ The Grand Old Man of Nashwaak ⇤

In nineteenth-century New Brunswick, one man held a lot of sway. Alexander Gibson was an entrepreneur, timber baron, railway magnate and mill operator. Known as the Grand Old Man of Nashwaak, or Boss Gibson, his mill town at Marysville, across the river from Fredericton, employed a huge workforce that ultimately passed most of its wages back to him. Gibson died in 1913, as one of New Brunswick's most wealthy and colourful businessmen.

Gibson founded Marysville (named after his wife) in 1886. He erected brick duplexes for hundreds of his workers. His cotton mill has been converted to government offices, and the duplexes are still standing. In 1997, Marysville was designated one of Canada's last intact nineteenth-century mill towns, and named a National Historic District.

⇥ Royal tea at Barbour's emporium ⇤

The year of Canada's birth, 1867, is also the year one of the Maritime's most recognized food companies began operation when brothers George and William Barbour opened a food emporium in Saint John. Well-known today for is delicious peanut butter and other goodies, Barbour's is perhaps best known for being the company that carries the famous King Cole Tea. Barbour's and King Cole Tea—both long-standing Maritime traditions.

The legacy of Clayton and Sons ⭠

In 1869, a tailor's widow named Mary Clayton, worked with her sons to begin a clothing manufacturing enterprise that, at its peak, employed five hundred women and men. Clayton and Sons Clothiers was eventually taken over by Mary's granddaughter, Louise, who rose to become president of the company. The factory was operated on the present site of Scotia Square in downtown Halifax. In 1904, the Claytons built a lovely summer home near what is now the entrance to one of Halifax's oldest communities, Clayton Park.

⭢ Fortune and tragedy at Beaconsfield House ⭠

Beaconsfield House in Charlottetown is one of the Maritimes' most beautiful Victorian mansions. It was built in 1877 for James Peake Jr., one of the Island's wealthiest merchants and shipbuilders. James and his wife Edith were grand hosts, and Beaconsfield shone for the Island's society and visiting royalty. But by 1879, just two years after building their dream home, the Peake family's world began falling apart. They lost two children to diphtheria, and when the country was hit with a depression they lost their fortune and Beaconsfield. Edith and her remaining children moved in with her parents, and James worked at odd jobs throughout Canada and the United States. Beaconsfield House is now home to the Prince Edward Island Museum and Heritage Foundation.

⭢ Prince Edward Island's welcoming shores ⭠

With its potential for agriculture, Prince Edward Island was seen as a good place to settle, especially by some early British immigrants. The nineteenth-century *European Immigration Gazette* wrote of the Island: "It is the Englishman's and the Scotsman's and the Irishman's friend—a shore for them to flock to when there is no food for them in their own country...If the poor in England did but know the advantages this Island holds forth, they would not stay and starve as they do."

⇝ A pain-free guarantee ⇜

Some of our ancestors may have shunned demon rum, but according to this advertisement in the October 6, 1888, edition of the *New Glasgow Enterprise*, they had access to more adventurous stimulants when they visited the dentist. The ad read: "Dr. Wolff, dentist. Office at his dwelling house, head of Provost and Archimedes streets New Glasgow. Painless extraction by use of Nitrous Oxide gas, Cocaine, etc. Durable artificial sets and fine fits guaranteed. Natural teeth carefully filled and cleaned."

⇝ Fire insurance in a flammable town ⇜

The earliest insurance company based in Nova Scotia was the Halifax Fire Insurance Company, begun in 1809. It operated in one room on Hollis Street, occupied by the secretary of the company. Its original directors met at the Exchange Coffee House on Upper Water Street. They helped bring about better fire protection in the town that consisted of mostly wooden buildings. In 1837, they gifted Halifax with its first fire engine. The new fire engine protected their investments, and saved them from paying out premiums to policy holders.

⇝ Wampum, pounds, and Halifax money ⇜

Over our long history, various forms of currency were used in the Maritimes. The North American First Nations people used a form of currency called wampum, made of shell beads, and they also traded in arrowheads and furs. Until the early part of the nineteenth century, money from all over the world was accepted as legal currency in the Maritimes. Early Maritimers used currency from Upper Canada, but mostly used French money when dealing with the French, and so-called Boston money when dealing with the British. They also dealt in Spanish coins. A form of currency (known as Halifax money) was issued shortly after that town's founding in 1749, and was recognized as legal currency into the 1860s. Early banks actually minted and printed their own money, so the currency supply was very eclectic. Banking consolidation was needed, and in 1820, the Bank of New Brunswick was incorporated, which made it the first chartered bank in British North America.

Say cheese—the
↦ Maritimes' first studio ↤
photographer

William Valentine was a portrait painter who, on November 15, 1841, placed an ad in the *Saint John Morning News* announcing that he was newly returned from the New England states, and was offering the new "Photographic Likenesses by the Daguerreotype Process." The next year, he placed a similar ad in the *Halifax Times*. Valentine's photographic studios are believed to have been the first in British North America, and since he visited Prince Edward Island as a portrait artist, many assume he brought his camera equipment too, which would make him the first professional photographer to work in all three Maritimes provinces.

↦ Barrels of herring—on sale now! ↤

Elizabeth MacDonald, wife of Prince Edward Island Father of Confederation, Andrew MacDonald, recalled the following of Victorian Charlottetown: "The Town Crier...marched around Queen's Square ringing his bell, and crying at the top of his leather lungs, 'A sale on Pownal Wharf! The packet just brought 40 barrels of good herring to be sold at two o'clock. Oh Yes! Must be sold. Oh! Yes, at two o'clock!'"

✦ An end to tuberculosis on the Island ✦

According to the World Health Organization, tuberculosis is primarily an illness of the respiratory system, and is spread by coughing and sneezing. Each year, about two million people die from this curable disease. Fortunately, it is rarely seen in the Maritimes today, but in 1903 it was one of the nation's worst killers. In that year, Canada's first tuberculosis sanatorium was established in Kentville, Nova Scotia. For many years, people from all over the province travelled to "The San" to take the cure of rest, fresh air, and new forms of drug treatment. It wasn't until 1967, Canada's centennial year, that there were no deaths resulting from tuberculosis reported in the province of Prince Edward Island. What made this achievement so great? No other province had gone a full year without deaths from tuberculosis in the history of the nation.

✦ Sweet savings for sugar refinery ✦

The Nova Scotia Sugar Refinery, once located on the waterfront near Young Street in Halifax, began operations in 1880. It featured a ten-story filter house that was, at that time, the tallest structure in the Dominion east of Montreal. At peak times, the refinery had 120 employees working around the clock. The company had private capital, but was publicly subsidized with a supply of free water and an exemption from taxes.

✦ Success in a tin of sardines ✦

New Brunswick brothers Patrick and Lewis O'Connor began a fishing business in the 1880s. In 1889, they got into the canning business. They began with blueberries and clams, and eventually moved on to sardines, marketing their tinned goods under the Brunswick label. The company name was registered as Connors Brothers in 1893. Today, Connors is the largest producer of tinned sardines in North America.

Why are sardines packed so tightly into tins? It seems the oil they are packed in is more expensive than the fish. So, more fish, and less oil equals lower costs, and higher profit!

✒ Peruvian beer, Pepsen soda, and Tangerette ✒

In 1894, Simeon White of Sussex, New Brunswick, was having a well drilled on his land when the machinery struck strong-smelling mineral water. Simeon turned this mineral water into the basis of a thriving soft drink empire. From those humble beginnings, Maritime Beverages Limited grew. From the early days of making Peruvian beer, Pepsen soda, and Tangerette to the popular Sussex beverages that it produces today, Simeon White's vision of turning mineral water into delicious soft drinks is a true success story.

✒ Rules for early nurses ✒

The nursing profession is an honourable one indeed. It's a trying occupation, but I might venture to say, not as trying as when these 1887 rules for nurses were published. I first read them in Douglas Baldwin's *Popular History of Prince Edward Island*:

"In addition to caring for your patients, each nurse will follow these regulations:

+ daily sweep and mop the floors of your ward
+ keep an even temperature by bringing in coal for the day's work
+ report every day at 7 a.m. and leave at 8 p.m., except on the Sabbath when you will be off from noon to 2 p.m.
+ graduate nurses in good standing with the Director of Nurses will be given an evening off each week for courting purposes...
+ any nurse who smokes, drinks liquor, gets her hair done at a beauty shop or goes to dance halls will give the Director of Nurses good reason to suspect her worth, intentions and honesty."

Furniture made
＞ of orange crates and ＜
imagination

In the 1930s and early 1940s, the Nova Scotia Wooden Ware company in Queens County, Nova Scotia, produced thousands of wood-veneer boxes for the Sunkist Orange Company. They called these containers orange crates. These same crates would be sent back to Nova Scotia filled with oranges, and when emptied, they were put to use as storage boxes, bureaus, and vanity tables in Maritime homes. My first dresser was an orange crate! My mother would take two crates, space them about a metre apart, and place a board across the top. A length of fabric thumbtacked around the edge of the board created a functional, if frilly, bedroom bureau or desk.

＞ The Maritimes' first Mi'kmaq teacher ＜

Born in Digby County in 1916, Elsie Charles Basque, was the first Mi'kmaq to receive a teaching licence from the Nova Scotia Provincial Normal College. The year was 1937. She taught in several schools in Nova Scotia, and finished her career with the Boston Indian Council. She returned to Nova Scotia to enjoy her retirement. Elsie Basque—a Canadian education pioneer.

＞ The early bird gets the … free rum? ＜

When Michael Francklin (Franklin), who eventually became Nova Scotia's governor, arrived in Halifax in 1752, he asked a boatman for advice on the best way to make money. He was told to open a rum shop and sell only the best. Well, he did, and advertised through the town crier: "Free rum to all, before 8 o'clock in the morning every day except Sunday, for one month." He became a very wealthy man!

→ A mid-week day of rest ←

In the early 1950s, New Brunswick folk song collector Louise Manny made regular Wednesday afternoon broadcasts featuring local singers (either live or recorded) performing the traditional songs she found in the Miramichi area. She often told how men in the lumber camps would stop work on Wednesday afternoons to listen in. That would be the perfect time to broadcast the shows because, throughout most of the Maritimes, Wednesday afternoon was the traditional time for stores and businesses to be closed. In fact, I can remember how many stores in the rural Maritimes continued to close their doors for business on Wednesdays well into the 1970s.

→ Spoolwood for Scots ←

Nineteenth- and early-twentieth-century woodsmen cut millions of trees for lumber and pulp, but they also cut thousands of birch trees for what they called spoolwood. In the days before thread was sold on plastic spools, millions of wooden spools were made each year. The Maritimes supplied many mills, such as the one in Newcastle, New Brunswick, that made thread spools for J. P. Coates Limited in Glasgow, Scotland.

→ Strippers and twisters ←

In a brief newspaper article for the *Guardian's* special issue celebrating the 150th anniversary of the founding of Charlottetown, Ivan Dowling explains how his father Al, worked as a "twister" while he proudly boasted of working as a "stripper." You see, in the 1920s, both father and son worked for Riley's Tobacco Factory in Charlottetown making chewing tobacco. Al's job was to twist the combination of leaf tobacco, licorice, rum, and other secret ingredients into the figs or twists of chewing tobacco. On school holidays, young Ivan would be hired to prepare the leaves for his father by stripping the soft leaf from the woody stem.

⤍ The sole of the Maritimes ⤌

The Amherst Shoe and Boot Factory sprang to life along with Canada in 1867. An amalgam of several businesses in Amherst, this factory produced a range of men's and women's sturdy work boots and fashionable shoes. By 1916, with a branch factory in Halifax, the company generated revenues in excess of one million dollars per year. World War One brought increased production and sales, but growing hard times crippled the Amherst Shoe and Boot Company and it closed in 1927.

⤍ Spruce-beer brewers apply within ⤌

The saying, "time changes all things" is very true when it comes to occupations. Many of the early pioneers to the Maritimes brought skills most of us don't possess. Here's an interesting example—a tally of the occupations of a group of thirty-eight settlers who came to Campobello Island with William Owen in 1770 listed the regular occupations of housemaid, blacksmith, barber, seaman, and potter, but also lists armourer, net weaver, husbandman, ship caulker, brick-moulder, pot-ash burner, cooper, claycaster, and spruce-beer brewers. Not many résumés today list spruce-beer brewing experience.

⤍ True love on the job ⤌

During the last two centuries, hundreds of small and large lumber camps and mills operated in Maritime Canada. The bulk of these were found in northern New Brunswick, and the southern and eastern ends of Nova Scotia. These camps provided work for thousands of men, and in quite a few cases, women too. I've never encountered any documented example of a female woods-worker, but many women and girls as young as twelve years old, worked as cooks and cook's assistants, or "cookies." My great-grandparents, Cora and Edward Burns ran a cookhouse on the St. Mary's River in Nova Scotia, and also employed their daughters as "cookies." It was at this camp that my grandmother Maxine, met a young woodsman named Ernest MacKay and the rest—as they say—is history. Well my history, at least!

⇝ Les filles de l'Acadie ⇜

At the same time, dozens of lobster factories dotted the shores on the Northumberland Strait between Pugwash and Tatamagouche. Canning lobsters was very labour intensive. The female workforce that handled the delicate meat extraction was mostly made up of Acadian women from the northern part of New Brunswick. These *filles de l'Acadie* made up a highly skilled seasonal workforce in an era when few women worked outside of the home.

⇝ I.W.K.'s legacy ⇜

Izaak Walton Killam was born in Yarmouth in 1885. He showed an early aptitude for financial matters, and quickly rose to prominence as one of Canada's most successful entrepreneurs. At one time he was the wealthiest man in Canada. He was also a man who shunned the spotlight. His biographer, Douglas How, called his work on Killam *A Very Private Person*. Izaak died in 1955, but his widow Dorothy, left several legacies to his native province, including the highly recognizable five-million-dollar endowment to support the Izaak Walton Killam Hospital for children.

⇝ The last of the pit ponies ⇜

For many years, horses were used in Nova Scotia's mines to transport men and ore. They were known as pit ponies, and often came from wild stock captured on Sable Island. Although most pit ponies were replaced with machinery by the 1940s, as late as 1978 two horses named Queenie and Donna worked the pits in the Drummond Mines at Westville.

✣ Faith, farce, and foam on Argyle Street ✣

Argyle Street is one of Halifax's most famous and popular locations. Although the spelling has changed, it is named in honour of the Duke of Argyll, who held the title of Keeper of the Great Seal of Scotland when Halifax was founded in 1749. The busy street boasts some of Halifax's oldest buildings and businesses, including St. Paul's Anglican Church and the Neptune Theatre, which, in 1915, began life as a vaudeville house known as The Strand. Argyle Street is also the location of the Seahorse Tavern, which opened its doors in 1948. This makes it Halifax's oldest operating tavern.

✣ Dr. Gesner's notes for newcomers ✣

In the early years of the nineteenth century, the government of New Brunswick was eager to discover more about its natural resources, especially the potential for developing coal reserves. With that goal in mind the province hired Nova Scotian scientist and inventor Abraham Gesner to take on the job of provincial geologist—the first such position in British North America. Dr. Gesner did make some interesting and controversial discoveries including the mineral albertite, which proved not to be the great coal-producing material he had thought it would be. Still, this man who would win fame as the inventor of kerosene contributed greatly to his province, and compiled the work *New Brunswick with Notes for Immigrants* (1847) that helped bring new immigrants to this part of the Maritimes.

✣ Time for a new job ✣

The man employed to clean the snow and ice off the hands of Halifax's Old Town Clock in the days before the face was covered with protective glass had to perform a daring task. Local lore says that to carry out his duties, the clock-keeper had to hang with a rope around his waist while his wife held him secure at the other end. It was a risky occupation if they'd had an argument earlier in the day!

→ **Mamie Moran and the Mount** ←

Born in Massachusetts in 1870, Mamie Moran decided on a religious life and became a Sister of Charity. In 1889, Mamie, now known as Sister Mary Evaristus, came to Halifax, and after numerous years of study locally and abroad, she petitioned and won the right to establish Mount Saint Vincent College in 1925. Now known as Mount Saint Vincent University, it was the first college in Canada to award credentials in arts and secretarial sciences.

→ **Guiding the way** ←

The Halifax School for the Blind was incorporated May 7, 1867 to help blind children in Nova Scotia, but didn't begin taking students until 1871. In 1873, a dynamic man named Charles Frederick Fraser, who was left blind after a childhood accident, became superintendent of the school. Fraser ran the school for fifty years. Under his direction, children from New Brunswick and Prince Edward Island became eligible for admission in 1874. For his yeoman service, Charles Fraser was knighted in 1915 by King Edward VII. Not one to rest, three years later he founded the Canadian National Institute for the Blind.

→ **New norms in New Brunswick** ←

Lieutenant Colonel Joseph Gubbins, British officer (and snob) was stationed in New Brunswick in 1811, and wrote of his observations on the early settlements and lifestyle. He was amazed and scandalized at the ease with which the citizens adopted a more liberal lifestyle, ignoring the class system of Great Britain. His primary objection was that, "the poor are not educated to respect the rich as in Europe." He did have to admit that New Brunswick had few desperately poor people, and those who fell on hard times were more often than not helped out by their neighbours. He was astonished when an abandoned wife was not turned out of her home or put into debtor's prison.

⤏ Aye, aye, ma'am! ⤎

Between beginning her working career as a stage designer for the theatre and ending her professional life as a prison warden and activist for better conditions for inmates, Halifax native Isabel MacNeill also made history by serving her country in World War Two as the only female commanding officer in any of the Royal Navies. While commanding officer of HMCS *Conestoga*, Isabel also led the Women's Royal Canadian Naval Service, known as the WRENS. It is because of Isabel MacNeill we have the phrase: "A woman's place is in command!"

⤏ Bizarre bureaucracy ⤎

In the late 1840s, Sable Island was sometimes used as a shelter for the mentally ill, or as it was called then, a lunatic asylum. Since no such institution was formally set up on the mainland, special arrangements were made to ship certain poor individuals to the Graveyard of the Atlantic. In a stroke of bizarre bureaucracy, when government authorities found that one man had spent several years in this isolation, and was known to roam mad among the dunes and wild ponies, they wrote to the Island's superintendent suggesting he be permitted to remain on the Island in the role of schoolmaster or any other task seen fit by the superintendent.

⤏ Building Acadia, one pie at a time ⤎

Acadia University is the first and oldest Baptist institution of higher learning in British North America. Incorporated under its present name in 1841, it is said to have been built without money. You see, cash was not readily available in the early, lean years. Donations of building supplies came in from the three Maritime provinces—and even the housekeepers contributed by selling eggs and apple pies.

☞ An odour to make fleas flee ☜

Maritime lumber camps were often rife with bedbugs and lice. One senior logger quoted in Mike Parker's *Woodchips & Beans: Life in the Early Lumber Woods of Nova Scotia* suggested the best way to get rid of fleas was to put your clothes over a horse for a while, so that they would take on the smell from the animal. Apparently, fleas can't tolerate the smell of a sweaty horse and will leave you alone if that's what you smell like. I imagine just about any living creature would!

☞ "L is for the lice that over us creep." ☜

In traditional folk song parlance, alphabet songs were often a good way for sailors and lumbermen to sing about their lives. From a version I collected from Alex Hiltz of New Ross, Nova Scotia, comes this verse from the "Lumberman's Alphabet Song," once so popular throughout the Maritimes:

> I is for the iron marking our pine,
> J is for the jolly boys falling behind,
> K is for the keen edge our axes do keep,
> And L is for the lice that over us creep.

☞ A teacher's test ☜

Imagine attending a school where you are required to arrive ten minutes before the other students, and must sit in the back of the class when you do take your seat. Imagine that you are not allowed to speak to either your classmates or teachers, and that you have to wear a veil over your face. Such were the conditions imposed on Martha Hamm Lewis when she successfully fought to be the first woman to attend the Saint John Training School in 1849 in order to become a teacher.

❧ Dr. F., a dashing dentist ❧

Ah, the joys of visiting the dentist. Actually, today's dentists provide fine services that are virtually painless. I wonder about the effectiveness of the services of the dentist who placed the following notice in the *Saint John and Fredericton Royal Gazette* in 1830: "Nothing is more disgusting to the sight than a mouth filled with decayed teeth, or teeth crowded with tartar. Dr. F. Gourland, Surgeon Dentist...offers his services to the Ladies and Gentlemen of Fredericton...filling their cavities with either gold or silver leaves...extract[ing] with dexterity broken or decayed teeth, roots or stumps, and insert[ing] artificial ones in their places." The ad warned his potential patients that "Doctor F. does not intend to visit Fredericton again for a long time."

❧ A house built on, by, and for the Island ❧

Prince Edward Island is known as the Cradle of Confederation, and Province House in Charlottetown is where the genesis of Canada was hammered out. It is truly an Island-built structure, for when construction began in 1843 every part of the building was designed and built using Island manpower and supplies, with the exception of some stone from Nova Scotia. Even the interior furnishings were constructed by Island craftsmen. Perhaps most impressive is the fact that Isaac Smith, the man who designed the building and oversaw every aspect of its construction, had no formal architectural training. Mr. Smith also designed the official residence for Prince Edward Island's lieutenant-governor in 1834.

❧ Grace Annie Lockhart, B. Sc. ❧

New Brunswick native Grace Annie Lockhart holds a distinction unique among women in the British Empire. Born in 1855, she was a student at New Brunswick's Ladies Academy then furthered her education at Mount Allison College, which had only become coeducational in 1874. Mount Allison had originally been established as a school for Methodist men. On May 25, 1875, Grace Annie Lockhart was awarded a Bachelor's degree in science and English literature. With that, she became the first woman in the British Empire to earn a university degree.

⇥ Broken telegraph ⇤

Communication through technology has come a long way. Our ancestors certainly had fewer choices than we do today. So when their telegraph technology went down they lost a major form of communication. Take, for example, a notice in the Halifax *Acadian Recorder* for March 6, 1858, when they informed their readers that while moving a building, Thomas Dunlap of Truro broke the wires and severed all telegraph contact between New York and Montreal. The system failure lasted for an entire day, and the paper suggested that Mr. Dunlap be prosecuted and made to pay. He wasn't and he didn't!

⇥ Lights out—during the day ⇤

When the town of Amherst first got electric power in 1889, residents were not charged for the quantity of power used, but according to the number and location of their light bulbs. The cost was three cents for a light in the drawing room; seven cents for one in a lower hall; and a light in the kitchen set you back five cents a month. The electric company wasn't worried that its customers would leave the lights on all day. The power only came on from dusk 'til midnight.

My condo building, on Halifax's Spring Garden Road, had the distinction of being the first building east of Montreal to be completely powered by electricity, when it opened as an apartment complex in 1964. It seems Halifax likes being in the front of the pack when it comes to electricity technology. Some researchers suggest we hold the distinction of being the first city in North America to be lit entirely by electricity. The year was 1890.

New Brunswick is home to the Point Lepreau Nuclear Generating Station, but that province's early power outputs were substantially less grand. The first major power plant in New Brunswick was operated by the Saint John Electric Light Company. When it began production in 1884, the plant only produced enough energy to power six one-hundred watt light bulbs.

⤳ An egg-cellent invention ⤶

In the nineteenth century, a fellow from Prince Edward Island named Watson Duchemin made his living making pumps and blocks for the many sailing vessels being built on the Island. But, Watson had other interests, too. He was an inventor! He patented a form of roller-bearing to improve the standard wooden blocks used at the time. But his most interesting invention was a device for holding and transporting eggs. In 1871, he patented what he called Duchemin's Improved Egg Carrier. This consisted of a wooden rack holding individual cloth pockets for each egg. Twenty-four pockets made a flat, and the flats could be stacked. Sound familiar? Today, those cloth pockets have been replaced with cardboard but the concept remains the same—Duchemin's egg carrier has transformed into today's egg carton!

⤳ A travelling laboratory ⤶

Opened in 1962, the Bedford Institute of Oceanography in Nova Scotia is Canada's largest centre for ocean research, and is recognized as a world leader in oceanographic studies; however, Canada had an earlier marine research facility in New Brunswick. In 1893, the Canadian Commissioner and Inspector of Fisheries requested a marine biological station be established. He got his wish with a portable, sixteen-metre long laboratory that resembled a Pullman railway car. Its first location was near St. Andrews, New Brunswick, and in 1901, the station began being towed to various locations around the Maritimes.

⤞ Prince Edward Island calling ⤝

Telephone service began on Prince Edward Island in 1884, when an exchange line was set up in the Charlottetown law offices of Palmer and MacLeod at the corner of Great George and Richmond streets in the Union Bank Building. The following year the company was incorporated as The Telephone Company of Prince Edward Island. But off-Island telephone communications didn't take place until January 3, 1911, when the first interprovincial calls were made through a submerged cable from Wood Islands to Pictou, Nova Scotia.

⤞ Easy to reach ⤝

Having a difficult time remembering your telephone numbers now that you have home, office, and cell phones? It was quite a bit easier for Dr. Edwin E. Dickey when he advertised his practice in the *Wolfville Acadian* on April 8, 1904. His ad gave his location as "two doors east of the Manual Training Hall." His telephone number was simply 5.

⤞ Signalling all skaters ⤝

As you look out over Halifax Harbour near the Dartmouth Commons on Wyse Road, you can see a small signal light situated on Synott's Hill. It was moved there in 1907, but its original home was a far more interesting location. Before its relocation, the light served harbour navigation from atop the tower of the old skating and sports rink of the Chebucto Club, where the present Dartmouth Sportsplex stands. It was probably the only signal light at a skating rink.

⤞ Edison salutes Amherst ⤝

On July 31, 1907, H. J. Logam, a member of parliament, and chairman of the board of trade committee in Amherst, received the following telegram: "Permit me to congratulate your board of trade and Senator Mitchell on the inauguration of the first power plant on the American continent for the generation of electricity at the mouth of a coal mine and the distribution of the same to distant commercial centres. It is a bold attempt and I never thought it would be first accomplished in Nova Scotia where my father was born over one hundred years ago. Thomas A. Edison."

✦ Black gold in New Brunswick ✦

In 1859, a small quantity of oil was extracted from four wells near the New Brunswick community of Dover. They were among the first productive oil wells in North America.

In the year 1909, the cry of "oil" may well have been heard at Stoney Creek, near Moncton. Oil and natural gas were commercially extracted at this site until production was suspended in 1991. Then in 1998, new discoveries were made in the area, and interest in New Brunswick's potential for oil and natural gas production was renewed.

✦ Nova Scotia's newest island ✦

Sable Island has traditionally been considered part of Nova Scotia, but it wasn't until February 1, 1977, that the province signed an agreement with the federal government affirming Nova Scotia's claim to ownership. It was an important ruling because of the potential revenues from offshore natural gas fields. Nova Scotians sat back and hoped for the money to start flowing in with the gas. We got the gas—now we're waiting for that big financial burp!

✦ Cooking up a connection ✦

We tend to think of microwaves and the microwave oven as innovations of the 1960s, but the technology goes back to the 1940s. In 1947, Raytheon demonstrated the world's first microwave oven, and called it a Radarange. The technology was also used early on in the communications field, and on November 19, 1948, the Maritime Telegraph and

Telephone Company began the first commercial microwave link in the world, connecting Nova Scotia and Prince Edward Island.

❧ Educating by doing ❧

Maria Montessori was an Italian doctor and educator who developed a system of learning for children. Her methods, which, in part, look at how unconscious learning is nurtured and develops to a conscious level, are recognized the world over. Through a hands-on approach to education, children learn by doing—developing skills that allow them to think for themselves. The first Montessori school in North America was opened on April 7, 1900, in Baddeck, Nova Scotia.

❧ Books for every Islander ❧

Because of its relatively isolated location and low access to reading material, Prince Edward Island was chosen by the Carnegie Corporation as the test site for the development of a regional library system in 1933. They sent Nora Bateson to the Island, and by 1936 she had opened twenty-two branch libraries that supplied the demand for reading material among Island citizens. Communities too small for a local library worked with the local women's institute to make certain every Island citizen had access to library services. Because the Island's muddy roads could bog down a heavy bookmobile bus, the library's director created what she called the book car, a converted Chevy coupe with the trunk redesigned to hold portable shelves. The car was still light enough to get over Island mud, and allowed a mobile library to be set up anywhere in about two minutes.

❧ Machines that sing ❧

Business must stay current or die. That was true for some early Maritimes companies, including the Amherst Piano Works Limited that began manufacturing quality pianos in 1912. By 1913, they employed one hundred men and shipped pianos to Canada and the West Indies. After World War One, when times changed and new inventions, such as affordable recording machines, brought new musical tastes, the company also began producing the Cremonaphone Talking Machine.

⇝ *Blue Water* on the big screen ⇜

The photographs and writings of Frederick William Wallace are among the best records of the days of sail in the Maritimes. In fact, two of his novels, *Blue Water* and *Captain Salvation*, were made into feature films. *Blue Water* was released by Saint John's fledgling New Brunswick Films Limited in 1924, while *Captain Salvation* received the full Metro-Goldwyn-Mayer treatment in 1927. Sadly, copies of neither film have survived.

⇝ Television reaches the Maritimes ⇜

High-definition and wide-screen televisions are becoming the norm these days, and it's hard to imagine life without the all-seeing eye in our homes. With cable and satellite service, viewing choices are unlimited. Canada's first television station was launched at CBFT-TV in Montreal on September 6, 1952. A month later, on October 9, CJCB-TV in Sydney, Cape Breton, went to air, making it the eighteenth station in the nation and the first in the Maritimes.

Many communities in Germany were destroyed during World War Two, and postwar development and technologies were often slow to reach the country. One German immigrant to Canada told of arriving in Halifax in the 1950s. The family boarded the train for Montreal and, as they travelled through the towns they saw strange blue lights flickering in many of the windows they passed. Only later did they learn the lights came from television sets.

On February 17, 1958, Pope Pius XII designated Saint Clare of Assisi the patron saint of television. That was also the year the Canadian Broadcasting Corporation extended its microwave network from Victoria,

British Columbia, to Halifax and Sydney, Nova Scotia, making it the longest television network in the world.

→ Roadblocks for African Canadian teachers ←

Born in Fredericton, Mary Matilda Winslow entered the University of New Brunswick's Arts program in 1901 and graduated in 1905, earning top honours in her class. Although her qualifications were outstanding and should have allowed her to gain a teaching position in her native province, such was not the case. You see, Mary Winslow was the first African Canadian woman to attend a university in New Brunswick and at that time African Canadian educators were not hired for teaching positions in the province. Mary did teach for a time in Halifax, and eventually finished her professional career and her life in the United States.

→ A retirement home for computers ←

When I recently upgraded my computer system, I should have sent my old computer to a special retirement home in Annapolis Royal—Nova Scotia's only computer museum. Along with computers, the museum also features a collection of old video games and robots for your interest and amusement. It's a "real" museum, open during the summer for "real" visitors. Maybe they even have my old Tandy with the small screen and green type. Now I'm really dating myself!

→ Telegrapher's paralysis ←

The days of the telegrapher are gone, but, during the last two centuries thousands of Maritime men and women worked the telegraph keys to send out millions of messages. Many of these workers developed severe pains in their arms and wrists—a condition they knew as telegrapher's paralysis or glass arm. Today, we know a similar problem that results from the overuse of a computer keyboard. We call it carpal tunnel syndrome.

⇥ Smoking success for the Macdonald brothers ⇤

Prince Edward Island native William Macdonald was born in 1831, and grew to be one of the richest men in the colonies. In 1858, he and his brother Augustine started a tobacco company in Montreal. They christened the new company McDonald Brothers and Co. Tobacco Manufacturers. In 1866, William changed the name to W. C. McDonald Tobacco Merchants and Manufacturers. Then, after being knighted by Queen Victoria in 1898, he added the letter *a* to McDonald and MacDonald Tobacco began using a heart-shaped logo with the company slogan "tobacco with a heart." Many Canadians will remember the distinctive cigarette package with the highland lassie on the cover. But, here's is an interesting sidebar to this bachelor entrepreneur's life. William couldn't stand the smell of tobacco, and forbade smoking in his presence. Funny world, isn't it?

⇥ Dangerous and unclean habits ⇤

In 1870, Sackville, Nova Scotia entrepreneur, William Grove, died at age 51 of what was termed tobacco heart. According to the *The American Heritage Stedman's Medical Dictionary*, the term is an old one indicating "a rapid, irregular heart rate resulting from excessive use of tobacco."

Statistics show there is a marked increase in the use of snuff and chewing tobacco among Maritime teens. We now have proof that this alarming trend can lead to throat and mouth cancer, but our forebearers had other concerns about the practice of taking a "chaw." In 1900, the Halifax and Dartmouth Council of Women passed a resolution against what they called "the dangerous and unclean habit of expectorating in public places." This wasn't because of health concerns, but was in response to the many men who chewed tobacco and then let the juices fly where they may.

✦ Mi'kmaq creativity ✦

Archeological evidence dating back over three thousand years provides examples of clay cooking and storage vessels being made and used by the Mi'kmaq. Without the use of a potter's wheel, Mi'kmaq artists used the clay-coil method to fashion pots and used crushed shells to give the fired pieces a durable finish.

If you are fortunate enough to own a piece of Mi'kmaq quill work, you have a fine piece of art. Because of their frequent use of porcupine quills to decorate boxes and clothing, the Maliseet people, who were neighbours of the Mi'kmaq, referred to them as porcupine people.

✦ A "holsum" idea ✦

Ben's Bakery Limited has roots dating back to the 1790s when Scottish immigrant Alexander Moir began selling his wife's bread to the Halifax garrison stationed at Citadel Hill. A bakery established by Alexander's great-grandson, Benjamin, opened on Pepperell Street in Halifax in 1907. Many times I was sent to the store to get a loaf, and thousands of other Maritime kids were raised on the famous Ben's "Holsum" bread.

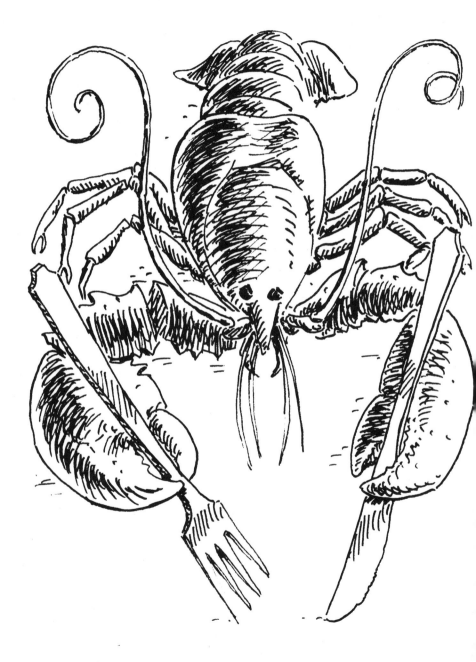

⟣ CHAPTER EIGHT ⟢
MARITIME MEALTIMES

⟶ Which came first, *le poulet* or *le poule*? ⟵

Acadian words often differ from the French language used in the mother country. For example, my wife's Acadian grandmother, Christina May (Richard) Brown, was born in 1895 at Charlos Cove, in Guysborough County, Nova Scotia. She used to tell us that the word *poulet* was reserved for the best chicken, which was only served when the priest or some other important guest was present. The rest of the time, the family ate an old hen past her laying days, and called it *un poule*.

⟶ Eat and run ⟵

Robert Harris, Prince Edward Island's most famous artist, and the man whose painting immortalized the 1864 meeting of the Fathers of Confederation in Charlottetown, was a fifteen-year-old member of the musical band that entertained at a grand banquet in the Colonial Building when Canada's founding fathers met to discuss the union. Seems he came home with more than memories because his mother recorded in her journal that "one of the gentlemen told him to fill his pockets, so the following morning he had a store of good things to distribute around the house."

⟶ The Maritime staff of life ⟵

In fifteenth-century Nova Scotia, Samuel de Champlain reported that his Mi'kmaq guests relished the bread made by the French cooks, and would eat great quantities at the feasts of the Order of Good Cheer. Early European settlers in the Maritimes baked some of their breads in hot sand, and the Acadians baked their bread in large outdoor ovens attached to one side of a house. Barley bread was once very popular in Nova Scotia's Lunenburg County, while Celtic settlers enjoyed Irish soda bread or Scottish bannock. And brown bread and molasses with baked beans was once a Saturday night staple on many a Maritime table.

An old Maritime folk belief said if you turned a loaf of bread upside down it would upset a ship at sea. In Shelburne County, Nova Scotia, it was believed to bring bad luck if a loaf of bread was turned upside down in the pan immediately after it was taken out of the oven. Bread was also thought to bring good luck. It was believed that if you saved a bun from a batch of bread baked on Good Friday, it would dry up, get hard, and keep forever. As long as you kept it, your house would never burn and the ship you sailed in would never sink.

⸭ Ninety-eight thousand gallons of rum ⸮

Rum continues to be a popular drink in the Maritimes, but its consumption today is nothing compared to the quantities some of our ancestors imbibed. In his book *Historic New Brunswick*, Dan Soucoup writes about the first vessel built on the St. John River. It was called the *Betsy*, and was launched in 1769. It's hull and all wooden components were made of local wood, but its sails and rigging were imported from Massachusetts. But, what I found particularly interesting is that in just one voyage to the West Indies, the *Betsy* returned to its home port of Saint John with ninety-eight thousand gallons of rum.

⸭ Lost and misplaced cows ⸮

Sadly, newspaper advertisements for lost animals are all too common. Cats and dogs are cherished members of the family and sorely missed when they are lost, but, years ago, a lost cow could mean great hardship. Cows supplied milk and cheese to hungry pioneer families, so the urgency of this notice in the Prince Edward Island *Royal Gazette* of November 20, 1832, can be well understood: "STRAYED, about three months since, from the New Glasgow Road, a dark brown COW, with a little white on her back, and white on the tip of the tail, the tops of her horns cut off, seven years old. Whoever will give information where she may be found, will be rewarded for their trouble, by applying to Thomas Walsh or to TERENCE O'BRIEN. New Glasgow Road, 15 miles from Charlotte-Town."

Not everyone was enamoured with cows. Halifax's Citadel Hill has the reputation for being the most visited National Historic Site in the nation. The fortress and museum is a must-see for visitors to the capital city. It dominates the skyline in many places. Today it is enjoyed by locals who coast its snowy slopes, sunbathe on its grass, and fly kites high above the city. How times have changed. All these activities would have been hard to do back in 1873, when Halifax newspaper the *Acadian Recorder* complained that "people are denied the privilege of walking, sitting, standing on the Citadel...because of a few cows which are quartered on the grounds in question, all access to this salubrious spot is forbidden to people."

⤳ A good chaw ⤶

As far back as I can remember, my grandfather Ernest MacKay used chewing tobacco. His brand was Pictou Twist. The manufacture of this "delicacy" started in the early nineteenth century when Archibald McKenna of Ireland began making chewing tobacco in the town of Pictou, Nova Scotia. The business changed hands several times, but the product remained the same. I was told that what made Pictou Twist so unique was a special blend of ingredients rolled with the tobacco leaves, including molasses, licorice, and other secret things. I can't say, as I never tasted the stuff. But for my grandfather, it was a special treat.

⟫ Soup served by helping hands ⟪

A number of organizations offer meals to folks in need. It is a service with a long history. After the War of 1812, Nova Scotians experienced an economic depression, and many hundreds were in need of aid. That's when Michael Tobin, a merchant, and Samuel Cunard, shipping magnate, administered a soup kitchen in Halifax that provided food to five hundred people a day.

⟫ Sweet treats ⟪

Our Victorian ancestors sure knew a thing or two about candy. Just look at some of the varieties advertised for sale by Alex McKenzie of Charlottetown in 1861: "fruit drops, barley sugar, sugar almonds, French cordial beans, chocolate faces, caraway comtits, cinnamon string, polka drops, pearled sugar, sugar marbles, clear toys, and peppermint drops." Alex also sold soap, crackers, raisins, spruce chewing gum, brooms, and plaster of Paris.

⟫ Lobster, champagne, and national unity ⟪

The Fathers of Confederation certainly ate well during their first meetings in Charlottetown in 1864. One luncheon included "champagne cooled in tubs of ice; jellies flanked with Charlotte Russe and fragile meringues quivering on the long damask draped serving tables. Lobster boiled and chilled and piled on great platters, the gleam of freshly polished glasses, flowers and fruit, welcomed thirty-three hungry and elated men at three in the afternoon."

⟫ Eating well, Acadian style ⟪

Here's an old Acadian cookie recipe that's probably not used much these days—it's for *galette au petit-lard de loup marin*, which means seal blubber cookies. The fat in these cookies, made using a simple sugar cookie dough, is replaced with rendered blubber from the harp seal. In an age when seals were used to provide both food and clothing, Acadian families probably developed quite a taste for these cookies.

In most areas of the Acadian Maritimes, the French language spoken by local inhabitants carries a distinctive regional patois. In the district of Clare, along the Fundy shore, retired educator Felix Thibodeau has compiled many examples of a language that arrived in Nova Scotia with early settlers from the Poitou region of France. One example is the pronunciation of *pain*, the word for bread. The older, Acadian version sounds more like "pon," pronounced so that it rhymes with son. Another delightful tidbit of Acadian food nomenclature is the phrase used to describe the delicious glassworts known in Maritime English as samphire or sandfire greens. These bright green succulents grow along beaches, shorelines, and mud-flats. When steamed or lightly fried, they are considered by many, me included, to be a great delicacy. The stems have clusters of tiny bulbs on them, which is probably the reason the Acadians call them *tétines de souris* or mouse nipples!

✤ Strawberries in December? Grapes in March? ✤

Sure, our local grocery stores are full of them. We've become so used to eating seasonal fruits all year that younger generations don't remember when tropical or out-of-season fruit was a rare treat. For some wealthy nineteenth-century Haligonians, it was not so rare a treat either. William Cunard's vast estate overlooking the Northwest Arm was once famous for its greenhouses, where winter strawberries and a variety of grapes were grown and served to lucky dinner guests.

✤ Raising a glass to the end of prohibition ✤

Maritimers like a drink now and then, so it's no wonder prohibition wasn't on their list of good things. While Quebec was the first province to abolish prohibition in 1919, followed by British Columbia in 1920, we took our time catching up. Even then, like in most of Canada, sales of liquor were controlled by provincial liquor boards. Manitoba led the pack in 1923. In 1927, New Brunswick became the first Maritime province to have government-controlled liquor sales, followed by Nova Scotia in 1930. Prince Edward Island finally gave up official prohibition in 1948.

⇥ Fly beer ⇤

Once, when I was twelve, I tried to make homemade beer. My buddies and I concocted this brew in the woods near our homes. My mother unknowingly contributed to my early career as a brewmaster by giving me the five pound bag of sugar used in the mix. (I told her I was making fudge.) Our beer blew up as I was sampling it, so I guess you could count my attempt as a failure, though my brew was probably no worse than some made by Maritime woodsmen. They'd make the beer in open kegs that collected forest debris and flies—in fact, the brew was commonly known as fly beer.

⇥ The nectarine's nebulous origins ⇤

St. Andrews is one of New Brunswick's, and Canada's, most scenic towns. During the last two centuries, many wealthy families have moved there for its beauty and recreational facilities. One such fellow, Sir William Van Horne, was the builder of the Canadian Pacific Railway. His estate, called Covenhoven, was palatial and boasted extensive gardens. He even imported a famous gardener from Kew, England, named Henry Clarke. It has been suggested that while he was a gardener at Covenhoven, Mr. Clarke crossed a peach with a plum and invented the nectarine. Most scientists agree the nectarine originated in China as a genetic variant of the common peach, but I'll not get into the argument as to whether Mr. Clarke did or did not create the nectarine in New Brunswick.

❧ Succulent seaweed ❧

Dulse. It's that salty, chewy seaweed so popular with Maritimers that is now finding it way into gourmet shops and health food stores, and why not? By weight, it has 75 percent as much vitamin C as an orange. So where is the best place to find this delicacy? Most folks agree it's along the shores of Grand Manan Island in the Bay of Fundy.

❧ Inexhaustible fish stocks run dry ❧

Large and bony, but with delicious flesh, shad is considered by many Maritimers to be a real delicacy. Shad were once prolific in the Bay of Fundy, and during the last decades of the nineteenth century, millions were salted and packed into barrels for market. One nineteenth-century description of the number of shad stated "that the supply is inexhaustible is plain to everyone," but by the twentieth century, their numbers, like many of our fish stocks, had been greatly diminished.

❧ Bring your own bowl ❧

In my books, any time is a good time for ice cream or gelato! My wife and I once paid almost eight dollars each for a refreshing gelato near the Colosseum in Rome, so here's a good deal I'd like to see return. It comes from the recollections of Dartmouth historian Edith Rawlings in the book she co-authored with the late Ian Forsyth titled *A Goodly Heritage: Memories of North End Dartmouth, Early 1900s.* Edith remembers a time when you could buy ice cream in bulk. If you took your own dish to the store, you got six scoops of ice cream for a quarter. Scoops were normally five cents each, but you got an extra scoop just for bringing your own bowl.

❧ Haymaker's switchell ❧

When I was a kid in Sherbrooke and haymaking time came around, I remember a drink made especially for this occasion. Known in many places in Nova Scotia as haymaker's switchell, one popular recipe found in Hattie Perry's book, *Old Days, Old Ways*, lists the following ingredients:

2 cups of brown sugar
1 cup molasses
1 1/2 cups of vinegar
1 teaspoon ginger
1 gallon water

This mixture was often left in the well to cool, and provided a refreshing drink that cut the dust from the job of haying.

⇥ Butterine and other so-called foods ⇤

Even if you're not certain exactly what all of the ingredients in your food are, at least they have to be listed on the package. This wasn't so in 1897 when the St. Andrews, New Brunswick, newspaper *The Bay Pilot*, published the following notice about various substances being added to the produce available to Canadians: "Analysts have tested 813 samples of food, and found 271 adulterated...one third of the whole....Butter, is made up of meat fats...coloured and printed and sent to market as the genuine article. [It's called] Butterine. Tea, is so cooked up and doctored by spurious mixtures that "cheap Teas' have little or no tea in them. Milk, sold in cities [is] largely adulterated—out of 176 samples, 70 were found tampered with. As it is, one needs have the appetite of a vulture and the stomach of a cormorant, to eat and digest such a mass of adulterations, called—Food!"

⇥ Donair capital of the world ⇤

Folks who come from away are often puzzled by the ubiquitous culinary delight known as the donair. Similar to a Greek gyro, the meat and pita combination with its accompanying sweet sauce, is perhaps the most uniquely Haligonian dish we have. There is some argument over who invented the donair, but many sources attribute it to Peter Kamoulakos of Bedford, who served the first one in 1972. At any rate, they caught on— now Halifax proudly owns the title of donair capital of the world.

CHAPTER NINE

UNIQUELY MARITIME

✦ Blue jays on the ballot ✦

During Environment Week in 1976, the citizens of Prince Edward Island held an important election. They chose the brilliant azure blue jay as the province's official bird, and the role was made official during the 1977 session of the legislative assembly. With its blue-crested head feathers and bold black and white markings on its a vivid blue body, the blue jay is one of Canada's most beautiful birds. This colourful, and sometimes noisy, bird resides year-round on the Island. It is also featured on Prince Edward Island's provincial coat of arms, where it sits atop the shield holding an oak leaf, a symbol of the island's ties with Great Britain, in its beak.

New Brunswick adopted the black-capped chickadee as its provincial bird in 1983. Nova Scotia's bird is the osprey, adopted in 1994. While the blue jay and the black-capped chickadee both stick around for our Maritime winters, the osprey flies south to warmer climes.

✦ Bird Day ✦

According to Acadian tradition, the first Monday after Easter is known as Bird Day. It was the time when farmers went to church to pray that birds wouldn't come and eat their new crops, and causing a poor harvest in the fall.

✦ Johnny Woodboats ✦

Some regions in the Maritimes have developed unique styles of boats. The St. Mary's River in Nova Scotia has the river punt and the Cape Islander from Cape Sable are just two such examples. On New Brunswick's St. John River it is the St. John River Boat. First built in the late eighteenth century, these hardy vessels were designed to carry lumber. These two-masted ships which featured a snub-nosed bow, were built for carrying heavy loads rather than for speed. Although they were primarily used for river work, some of these odd-shaped vessels did engage in coastal trade in New England. The Americans nicknamed them Johnny Woodboats.

⇥ A royal flush ⇤

Members of the British royal family have been visiting the Maritimes for centuries—longer than any other part of the nation. Although Canada was formed during her reign, Queen Victoria never ventured to our shores. Some of her sons and her daughter did though. In 1879, Victoria's daughter, Louise, came to Canada with her husband, who had been appointed Governor General. When she visited Charlottetown in August of that year, Louise caused a small scandal because she chose to remain on board the royal yacht instead of enjoying the hospitality at Old Government House. Can't say I blame her. The yacht had something the viceregal residence didn't—a flush toilet.

⇥ A fitting farewell ⇤

I've been to many funerals, and each one is unique to the individual it honours. Some are very sad, others uplifting. Some are even full of laughter. I know of funerals conducted at sea, and mass funerals held in great halls. Perhaps the most unique funeral I've ever heard of was the April 16, 1909, funeral of W. D. Prendiville, superintendent of the Halifax Electric Tramway Company. His funeral was conducted on a tram car.

❧ Treasure island ❧

Tiny Isle Haute in the Bay of Fundy has a reputation of being home to buried treasure. Lots of islands do, but this spot has earned its reputation. Of the treasures that were said to have been taken from the island, the most famous was in 1952 when the Halifax *Chronicle Herald* posted the headline: "Reports Treasure Find Near Advocate Harbour." American treasure hunter Edward Rowe had discovered a human skeleton, and eight Spanish and Portuguese coins.

❧ UNB firsts ❧

In 1785, a year after New Brunswick was created, the United Empire Loyalists who had petitioned for it to be a separate colony, founded the University of New Brunswick (UNB). It is the oldest public university in North America. It's not surprising that UNB has several other firsts to its credit—Sir Howard Douglas Hall is the oldest university building still in use in Canada, and the Brydone Jack Observatory, established in 1851, is Canada's oldest observatory.

❧ Halifax welcomes Earl Grey ❧

On December 10, 1904, Halifax welcomed Earl Grey, his wife Countess Grey, and their two daughters as they made their way from London, England to Ottawa where Earl Grey was to take over his duties as the new Governor General. The swearing-in ceremony didn't take place at Rideau Hall, but in the red chamber at Nova Scotia's Province House.

❧ The turtle and the tourist ❧

Folk stories of the boastful American tourist are common in the Maritimes. One collected by Helen Creighton in Mahone Bay is of a Canadian and an American who were travelling together. The American was boasting that everything was bigger and better in the States, and the Canadian decided to put an end to the argument. He got a turtle and slipped it in the American's bed. When the bedclothes were turned back the American gazed at the turtle and asked, "What is this?" The Canadian replied, "That's a Canadian bedbug—can you do any better than that?"

⇥ Modified for the Maritimes ⇤

Martello towers were eighteenth- and nineteenth-century military structures designed to protect British colonial coastal areas from the threat of sea attack by Napoleon. They were constructed of stone, and were circular in shape with a flat roof on which artillery could be mounted. The eleven Martello towers in British North America were originally built with specially adapted removable cone-shaped roofs to protect against snow. The first of these adapted structures was built in the 1790s in Halifax's Point Pleasant Park under the direction of Edward, Duke of Kent. The other-well known Martello tower in the Maritimes is the Carleton Martello Tower that overlooks the harbour of Saint John.

⇥ Mother Coo's dire predictions ⇤

Born in New Brunswick in 1833, Ellen Creighton Coo spent her married life in Pictou County, Nova Scotia. Ellen's predictions about mine disasters earned her the nickname Mother Coo. Some feared her; others respected her foresight. When she successfully warned of the 1880 Ford Pit explosion in Nova Scotia, her fame was sealed. Her warnings were taken seriously by many, and when she predicted another disaster, this time at Springhill in 1891, Mother Coo was once again correct in her prediction.

⇥ Discovering a dinosaur ⇤

The year was 1845, and a man on Prince Edward Island named Donald MacLeod was digging a well when he found a remarkable relict from the past. He didn't know it then, but he had discovered the partial fossil of a creature that predated the dinosaurs. The fossil was identified by Francis Bain, an Island son, farmer, and self-educated expert on PEI fossils, rocks, and natural history. It turned out to be the fossilized remains of Bathygnathus Borealis—a fancy name for what dinosaur lovers know as the sail-back dinosaur, because the beast would have looked like a large lizard with a huge sail on its back. Donald Mac-Leod's 1845 find is considered the first, and some say only, one of its kind on record.

Nova Scotian fossil hunter, Eldon George, is responsible for two of the most exciting discoveries of prehistoric fossils in the world. In 1984, at Wasson's Bluff in Parrsboro, Mr. George discovered the fossil of the world's smallest dinosaur, a creature roughly the size of a robin. That same year, he found the fossilized footprints of one of the largest dinosaurs to roam our region—a giant crocodile that would have spanned eleven metres from snout to tail.

✦ More than one magnetic hill ✦

Moncton's Magnetic Hill, where one's car seems to coast up an incline, is the Maritime's most famous locale for experiencing this optical illusion. Years ago, Nova Scotia also had a couple of places where this seemingly amazing feat occurs. Although said to be gone now, due to new highway construction, writer Will R. Bird once described a spot on the road to Cape Smokey in Cape Breton where tourists noticed that cars seemed to travel uphill without their motors running. Mr. Bird also noted a road from Canning to the Blomidon Lookout in the Annapolis Valley where locals said the illusion was even better than at the Moncton site: however, it seems the Moncton locale is the major existing attraction, which continues to amaze countless visitors each year.

✦ Marked with an X ✦

What do former prime minister Brian Mulroney, former premier of New Brunswick Frank McKenna, late filmmaker Dan Petrie, singer Raylene Rankin, and late sportscaster Danny Gallivan have in common? An X-Ring! St. Francis Xavier University in Antigonish is one of Nova Scotia's finest centres of higher learning. It has turned out great scholars, stunning vocalists, world leaders in the economic and political fields, and remarkable athletes. These graduates are easily identifiable if they wear the attractive gold ring with the large black X on its face. In fact, according to the university's publicity department, the X-ring is the third most recognized ring in the world. The top two are the Pope's ring and a Super Bowl ring. To be honest with you, I wouldn't know the difference between the two, but I can pick out an X-ring every time!

✦ Unique history and beauty ✦

Born in 1891, Nova Scotian author William Richard Bird was an early proponent of exploring the Maritimes for its own unique history and beauty. A veteran of World War One, Will began his writing career in 1928, and won national recognition for his reports on postwar Europe. But it is his writings about his native land that endeared him to Maritimers. Two of his most popular works are *This is Nova Scotia* and *Off-Trail Along the Fundy Shore*. Will R. Bird was an early travel writer, a staunch supporter of Maritime history, and a fine author.

Supernatural ships ✦ in the Northumberland ✦ Strait

The most popular supernatural tales about ships in the Maritimes feature fire ships or phantom ships. The Northumberland Strait seems to hold the record for the number of sightings. For example, a woman from Cape John, Nova Scotia, reported seeing a three-masted vessel gliding up the Strait while a raging fire streaked through its hull, and up into its rigging. Some say this phantom ship is a true supernatural vision, while others suggest it is an optical illusion caused by gas escaping from submarine coal fields.

In the mid-1980s, I was giving a series of folklore lectures to Parks Canada staff in New Brunswick, and was told by one of the guides that, while accompanying a group of tourists through Fundy National Park, they watched a burning ship in the Bay of Fundy.

⇝ The arrival of Gothic Revival ⇜

The city of Saint John can boast about having one of New Brunswick's, and indeed, North America's, earliest examples of Gothic Revival architecture. In 1825, construction began on Lloyd Johnson's design for Saint John's Anglican Church. It was embellished with stone spires a year later by Scottish-born architect John Cunningham. Designs in the neo-Gothic style were new in the early part of the nineteenth century and novel on this side of the Atlantic. Also of interest is that the church was built using ballast stone brought to New Brunswick in British ships.

⇝ Equality, *égalité* ⇜

New Brunswick holds a unique position among Canada's provinces. In 1982, the province's Constitution Act declared: "English and French are the official languages of New Brunswick and have equal status and equal rights and privileges as to their use in all institutions of the legislature and the government of New Brunswick."

⇝ Armouries architecture ⇜

In the 1950s when I was a kid in Halifax, my dad was a reserve infantry member of the Princess Louise Fusiliers. I was always excited to accompany him when he went to the huge stone armoury building on North Park Street. Its ancient-looking design featured turrets. Its vast, unobstructed interior was a boy's dream place, and in my young imagination, it was a real castle. I didn't know then that the armoury's interior was cutting-edge when the building was erected in 1899. The roof is supported by a series of specialized Fink trusses that eliminates the need for obstructive columns and interior supports that would be in the way of soldiers doing marching drills. Today, the technology used to build the Halifax Armouries is the oldest surviving example of its kind in the world.

⇥ Tea time with the Queen ⇤

If you're a Maritime tea drinker you probably want your tea good and strong. In fact, some folks say the brew has to be boiled to be real tea. So, in an area famous for tea, what do you serve the Queen when she asks for a cuppa? Well, in a memoir published in the Charlottetown *Guardian* in 2005, Doug Boylan wrote that the Queen got an odd cup of tea during a 1964 visit to Prince Edward Island. Her Majesty was on the Island for the opening of the Confederation Centre of the Arts when, during a rest break, she asked for a cup of tea. Panic ensued—no one had planned on serving tea! That's when Mr. Boylan hurried to his office and made the Queen a cup of—get this—instant tea. He reported that as she was leaving the Queen thanked them for the "lovely cup of tea." Only in Canada!

The reigning constitutional Canadian monarch, Elizabeth II, first visited the Maritimes in 1951 as Princess Elizabeth, when she and her husband, the Duke of Edinburgh, embarked on a coast-to-coast tour of Canada. She made her first visit as Queen in 1957.

⇥ Calls for help ⇤

Workers who make up the 911 emergency service response teams play a vital role in seeking help for those in need. Their quick and professional responses have made the 911 system indispensable. On July 7, 1997, Nova

Scotia became the first province in Canada to offer the 911 emergency service to all its citizens. The Prince Edward Island 911 system came on board a year later. Here's a bit of cooperation unique to the Maritimes. New Brunswick, Prince Edward Island, and Nova Scotia are the only three provinces in Canada to offer border-to-border enhanced 911 services. Enhanced 911 service allows the 911 operator to see the phone number and address of a person calling from a landline in any of the three Maritime provinces.

⇸ A garden of floral emblems ⇷

The provincial flowers of the Maritime provinces are as diverse as the land itself. In 1901, the mayflower, a fragrant harbinger of spring, was named Nova Scotia's official blossom. The purple violet, sometimes used in jams and syrups, as well as in folk remedies for coughing, was adopted as New Brunswick's floral emblem in 1936 at the request of the provincial Women's Institute. And the lady's slipper was adopted as the provincial flower of Prince Edward Island in 1947. This orchid gets its name from the shape of its petals, which form a pouch that resembles a slipper. This handsome flower is considered endangered, and is a protected species—so look but don't pick!

⇸ The earliest RIP ⇷

In 1720, Samuel Douglas (Duglass) was serving with the British garrison at Fort Anne in Annapolis Royal when his thirty-seven-year-old wife, Bathiah, died. Her slate grave marker, situated just outside the fort in the garrison graveyard, features a grim-looking skull supported by wings. This grave decoration is commonly known as a death head. The marker, which has the distinction of being the oldest English gravestone in Canada, reads: "HERE LYES Y BODY OF BATHIAH DUGLASS, WIFE TO SAMUEL DUGLASS WHO DEPARTED THIS LIFE OCTO THE 1ST, 1720 IN THE 37 YEAR OF HER AGE." Established by the government of Canada in 1917, Fort Anne National Historic Site in Annapolis Royal is Canada's oldest national historic site.

❧ Evil spirits and infestations ❧

Superstitions are not always harmless. When a huge infestation of mice overran crops and fields on Prince Edward Island in 1750, some Island residents blamed a man named Pierre Perigord for causing the infestation. They believed he was an evil spirit. Legend says Pierre was killed and buried on St. Peter's Island in Hillsborough Bay.

❧ Rolling along the high seas ❧

During the 1930s, LaHave River Valley captain James (Andy) Publicover took his wife, Eledith, and their children on board with him as they sailed in the vessel *Lillian E. Kerr*. To give the children a sense of responsibility, son William was appointed mate, and daughter Dolly was assigned the title cabin-girl. To keep them amused, the children had musical instruments, games, and (best of all) roller skates. Imagine kids roller skating on the deck of a tall ship—I love that image!

❧ Worship in a wooden church ❧

Church Point, in the heart of Nova Scotia's Acadian district, is home to the largest wooden church in North America. Église Sainte-Marie is forty-one metres wide, and its spire reaches upwards for almost fifty-seven metres. The church's interior columns are actually made from whole trees covered with jute and plaster.

❧ Mussel mud ❧

Mussel mud is an idiomatic term for the gooey, dark substance gathered from the rich shellfish beds off the shores and tidal rivers of Prince Edward Island. It has been part of the Island's commercial economy since the 1860s. At one time, (when trains ran on the Island) rail cars called mud specials would be loaded to take this form of natural fertilizer to the inland farms of the Island. Mussel mud is rich in nitrogen, lime, and calcium, and according to Island farmers, you don't need a lot to fertilize the fields because this organic mixture is so rich in nutrients. At present, there are several commercial operators working on Prince Edward Island including sites at Orwell, St. Peter's Bay, and the Kensington area.

✤ Molly Kool, Master Mariner ✤

Hailing from Alma, New Brunswick, Molly Kool grew up helping her father on the twenty-one metre freighter he ran out of the Bay of Fundy. In a rare move for a woman in the 1930s, Molly decided to go for her officer's papers, and in 1939, became the first North American woman to earn a Master Mariner's license. The popular press claimed that Molly had "changed her hope chest for a sea chest," but Molly was a highly respected skipper, both in the Bay of Fundy and in European ports.

✤ Lolly ice ✤

According to Boyde Beck's book, *Prince Edward Island: An Unauthorized History*, lolly ice is a term used, since at least the 1850s, for ice in the Northumberland Strait. The ice forms into a mushy state, so that it's not thick enough to walk on or carry a boat over, but is too thick to row a boat through. Lolly ice. Now you know!

✤ Fundy fishing ✤

Aside from boasting of the highest and lowest tides in the world, the Bay of Fundy is also home to a traditional form of fishing that was practiced thousands of years ago by the Mi'kmaq and is still in use today. Long fences of poles intertwined with branches are placed in the water and used to capture fish as they move close to the Fundy shores. These traps, known as weirs, can stretch several metres out into the bay to capture herring and other species of fish. While some weir fishermen have re-placed the intertwined branches with netting, the process is unchanged. Fish swim against the fence and follow its path into a holding circle, and because these entrapments circle in on themselves, the fish remain in the weir. At low tide, the fisherman can tend the trap, which is left high and dry—the fish are stranded against the sides of the weir, or on the bottom of the Bay. In the old days, this was with horse and wagon, but now it is often done with a four-wheeler.

⤍ The doctor is in ⤚

Maria Louisa Angwin graduated and interned as a physician in the United States, but moved to Halifax where she set up a medical facil-ity devoted primarily to the care of the underprivileged. What makes this deed so remarkable is that Dr. Angwin began her practice in Nova Scotia in 1882, making her the first female physician licensed to practice medicine in the province.

⤍ Maritime flags ⤚

The flag of Nova Scotia is the oldest provincial flag in Canada and, perhaps, the oldest in North America. It was first authorized by the Charter of New Scotland granted in 1621 to Sir William Alexander by King James VI of Scotland. It was flown at the masthead of Nova Scotia ships until after Confederation in 1867, when it fell into disuse. It was revived again on January 19, 1929, by Royal Warrant, and continues to be a familiar icon to Nova Scotians.

Prince Edward Island adopted its flag in 1964 to commemorate the centennial of the Charlottetown Conference. New Brunswick adopted its flag a year later.

An Acadian knight

Born in Memracook, New Brunswick, in 1846, Pierre-Amand Landry would become one of Acadia's most outstanding sons. He was New Brunswick's first Acadian lawyer and the first Acadian to be elected to the provincial cabinet, earning that distinction in 1870 at age twenty-four. Twenty years later, he became the first Acadian county judge. Three years after that, he became the first Acadian to serve on the Supreme Court of King's Bench, and later took the office of chief justice. He died in 1916, shortly after becoming the first Acadian to be knighted, an honour he received from King George V. Pierre-Amand Landry—an Acadian pioneer.

A light that continues to shine

Canada's first lighthouse was erected at Louisbourg in 1734, but this country's oldest operating lighthouse is found at the entrance to Halifax Harbour on Sambro Island. Erected in 1758 and first lit in 1760, it holds the distinction of being the oldest lighthouse still in operation in North America.

Dawson City's Maritime connection

Two nineteenth-century Pictou, Nova Scotia, men made quite a mark in Canadian history. Sir William Dawson was Nova Scotia's first school superintendent, principal of McGill University, and first director of the Royal Society of Canada. His son, George M. Dawson, was director of the Geological Survey of Canada, and explored and mapped the Yukon in 1887. A town was named in George's honour—Dawson City.

Steep streets

San Francisco has a reputation for being a hilly city, but a few Maritime cities can boast some pretty steep streets, too. While Charlottetown and Fredericton are relatively level, Halifax has several steep slopes leading from Citadel Hill down to the harbour—just ask anyone heading home uphill after a night at the pubs. But the regional record goes to Saint John, New Brunswick. That city's King Street has an 8 percent grade, which means that over a distance of only two city blocks, it rises almost twenty-four and a half metres—that's about the height of an eight-storey building. It sure doesn't look it when you're standing there, but King Street is known as the steepest street in Canada.

☆ A welcome stranger ☆

Samuel Hawkins Napier was a Bathurst, New Brunswick, lad who trained as a sailor aboard the tall ships. However, when the 1850s gold rush hit in Australia, he changed occupations, and with his brother Charles, became a miner. Good thing, too! Sam Napier found the largest 95 percent pure gold nugget ever discovered in the Australian gold fields. This thing weighed over sixty-five kilograms. The brothers called the nugget "welcome stranger," and exhibited it in London before selling it. Sam moved back to Bathurst, eventually lost all his money, and died in 1902.

☆ Toussaint and cabbage soup ☆

November 1 is known as All Saint's Day. It was created by Pope Boniface IV in the seventh century to give recognition to all the saints and martyrs who didn't have a special day assigned to them. The Acadians know November 1 as a religious holiday called Toussaint. It is traditional to serve *soupe au chou*, or cabbage soup, sometimes left over from Halloween. Sister Mary Fraser of Antigonish County in Nova Scotia, collected this old belief about Toussaint: "On this day, the old people used to carry food to their poorer neighbours; [and] careful housewives would never throw water out of doors…for fear of harming the roaming spirits."

⇥ Halfway to the North Pole ⇤

The town of Stewiacke, Nova Scotia, is a pretty little community that is situated near the Shubenacadie Wildlife Park. It boasts some of the most exciting tidal-bore rafting in the world. The community is also proud to note (even on the town's official website) that they are halfway between the equator and the North Pole.

⇥ Canada's longest main street ⇤

Running for sixty kilometres along the Fundy shore of Nova Scotia, the district of Clare is home to thousands of Acadian citizens. Residents refer to the entire area as *la ville française*. The road that runs through the district, connecting villages such as Meteghan, Pointe de l'Église, St. Bernard and many more, has been called the longest main street in Canada.

⇥ The most liveable small town in the world ⇤

Thinking of moving to the Maritimes and looking for a good place to call home? Why not try Nova Scotia's Annapolis Royal? The town boasts a beautiful location on the Bay of Fundy, rich history as the cradle of European settlement in Canada, friendly people, and oh yes, according to the United Nations, who endorsed a program for recognizing the best small place to live in 2004—it's the most liveable small town in the world.

⇥ Canada's first monastery ⇤

There is an Augustinian monastery in Nova Scotia that is reputed to be the first monastery in Canada. In 1819, Father Vincent de Paul established a monastery near Tracadie, in what was later to be called, Monastery. It closed by 1897, but was re-established in 1903, and underwent numerous changes, including an influx of Augustinian monks escaping Nazi persecution in 1938. It is still in operation today, and the chapel is open to visitors.

↝ The very best in Miramichi ↜

Miramichi is one of Maritime Canada's most beautiful areas. It borders either side of New Brunswick's second-longest river, and its name is believed to be the oldest place name still in use in Eastern Canada. New Brunswick historian, William Francis Ganong, has suggested the word Miramichi is derived from a word used by the native peoples living by the St. Lawrence River called the Montagnais. These people were traditional enemies of the Mi'kmaq and Maliseet, and Ganong has suggested the word Miramichi may be translated to mean "the country of the bad people." That's certainly not a reflection on the folks living there today. The folks in the Miramichi have a special greeting that I think typifies Maritimers. They'll greet you with a hearty "How's she goin'?" To which you must reply, "The very best!"

↝ A delicious educational experience ↜

Can't get the kids to visit another museum? Here's one I bet they won't pass up! In St. Stephen, New Brunswick, you can take them to Canada's first chocolate museum. It shows the wonders and deliciously inspired history of the Ganong Brothers candy manufacturers. They first began creating treats in St. Stephen in 1873, and many believe the Ganongs created the first chocolate bar. In 1932, they became the first confectionary company to produce a heart-shaped box for their candy. That shape later became synonymous with Valentine's Day candy packaging. And there's a bonus many other museums don't offer—The Chocolate Museum has samples!

↝ A disappearing souvenir ↜

It seems a common enough icon of the region—the tourist driving home with the ubiquitous lobster trap on the roof of their car. For years, wooden lobster traps went off to become glass-topped coffee tables, or the main decorative feature of the family room, but the old wooden traps are now almost gone. Since their introduction in the 1980s, wire traps have become the norm. They last an average of fifteen years longer than the old kind, but somehow, they don't have the same charm!

⤳ From Venice to Halifax ⤲

In 1997, Halifax hosted the G7 Economic Summit of world leaders. Summit Plaza, which features a commemorative arch and performance area situated on the waterfront, is one legacy of the event. Adjacent to Summit Plaza is a commemorative statue given to the province of Nova Scotia by Italy in recognition of John Cabot's 1497 visit to our land. It features the Venetian lion, carved in marble. It is a replica of the carving on John Cabot's house in Venice. I remember walking by that house on a trip to Venice in 1996, and then recognizing the statue in my home city. Instantly, the world got a little smaller.

⤳ The land of Evangeline ⤲

Nova Scotia has been in the self-promotion business a long time. By 1869, the champions of the railways in the new province were using what was familiar to capture the attention of New England tourists. That's when the phrase "the land of Evangeline" made its debut. It made perfect sense—every New Englander studied Longfellow's poem in school. In 1891, thousands of copies of a book titled *Beautiful Nova Scotia* were sent across the border to promote our sights to the New England market. By 1895, the Dominion Atlantic Railway had produced a ninety-two page travel guide titled *The Land of Evangeline and the Gateways Therein*. Hundreds of copies were distributed to American schools. Good scheme—hook the kids, and they'll beg their parents to take them to Nova Scotia!

⟩ Happy New Scotland ⟨

Think today's tourist advertisements for Nova Scotia are boastful? How about this verse published in 1750 in the *Gentleman's Magazine* of London, England:

> Let's away to new Scotland where plenty sits queen,
> O' re as happy a country as ever was seen,
> And blesses her subjects, both little and great,
> With each a good house and a pretty estate.

The Nova Scotia Tourist Association was formed in 1898, and was taken over by the provincial government in 1925.

⟩ Uniacke's ha-ha keeps intruders at bay ⟨

The former estate of Richard John Uniacke, now a Nova Scotia Museum site, has evidence of a garden feature unique to Atlantic Canada. Archeological research has shown that the grounds around the mansion once held a ha-ha. Yep, a ha-ha. Seems in Georgian times, the folks living in mansions didn't want the animals grazing on their nearby property to come and eat the flowers close to the house, or leave droppings where the ladies might come in contact with them. To that effect, they built retaining walls in shallow ditches that were hidden from sight in the vista from the lawn, but also kept the animals at bay. In essence, a ha-ha is a sunken fence.

Along the Fundy shore at New Horton, New Brunswick, you'll find the Ha Ha Baptist Cemetery. The term "ha ha" also applies to the local bay and creek. A sign outside the cemetery tells visitors: "Legend has it that the Indians took the name 'ha ha' from the call of the loons."

✣ High praise for Cape Breton ✣

Alexander Graham Bell acquired land near Baddeck, Cape Breton, and built a home and studio at the estate he called Beinn Breagh (Gaelic for "beautiful mountain"). He had this to say about his adopted country: "I have travelled around the globe. I have seen the Canadian and American Rockies, the Andes, the Alps and the Highlands of Scotland, but for simple beauty Cape Breton outrivals them all." Enough said, Alex—I couldn't agree more.

⌐ BIBLIOGRAPHY ⌐

Atlantic Geoscience Society. *The Last Billion Years: A Geological History of the Maritime Provinces of Canada*. Halifax: Nimbus Publishing, 2001.

Avis, Walter S., ed. *Dictionary of Canadianisms on Historical Principles*. Toronto: W.J. Gage Limited, 1967.

Bagnell, Kenneth. *The Little Immigrants: The Orphans Who Came to Canada*. Toronto: Macmillan, 1980.

Baldwin, Douglas. *Land of the Red Soil: A Popular History of Prince Edward Island*. Charlottetown: Ragweed Press, 1998.

Baldwin, Douglas and Thomas Spira. *Gaslights, Epidemics and Vagabond Cows: Charlottetown in the Victorian Era*. Charlottetown: Ragweed Press, 1988.

Barris, Ted and Alex Barris. *Days of Victory: Canadians Remember 1939–1945*. Toronto: Macmillan, 1995.

Beck, Boyde. *Prince Edward Island: An Unauthorized History*. Charlottetown: Acorn Press, 1996.

Beck, Boyde and Edward MacDonald. *Everyday & Extraordinary: Almanac of the History of Prince Edward Island*. Charlottetown: PEI Museum and Heritage Foundation, 1999.

Beck, Boyde, Greg Marquis, Joan M. Payzant, and Shannon Ryan. *Atlantic Canada: At the Dawn of a New Nation*. Burlington: Windsor Publications, 1990.

Bell, John, ed. *Halifax: A Literary Portrait*. Lawrencetown Beach: Pottersfield Press, 1990.

Bennet, A. B. and Garnet Heislor. *Duelling Dories: 50 Years of International Dory Racing in Nova Scotia*. Tantallon: Glen Margaret Publishing, 2002.

Bishop, Tony. *The Gold Hunters Guide to Nova Scotia*. Halifax: Nimbus Publishing, 1988.

Bird, Will R. *Off-Trail Along the Fundy Shore*. Toronto: Ryerson Press, 1956.

Bird, Will R. *This is Nova Scotia*. Toronto: Ryerson Press, 1950.

Brebner, John Bartlet. *The Neutral Yankees of Nova Scotia*. Toronto: McClelland and Stewart, 1969.

Brown, Joe. *The View from Here: An Oral History of Eastern Passage, 1864–1945*. Shearwater: Shearwater Development Corporation, 1998.

Brown, Roger David. *Historic Cumberland County South: Land of Promise*. Halifax: Nimbus Publishing, 2002.

Bruce, Harry. *An Illustrated History of Nova Scotia*. Halifax: Nimbus Publishing and Province of Nova Scotia, 1997.

Bruce, Jean. *After the War*. Don Mills: Fitzhenry & Whiteside, 1982

Budge, Billy. *Memoirs of a Lightkeeper's Son*. Lawrencetown Beach: Pottersfield Press, 2003.

Bibliography

Carrigan, D. Owen. *Crime and Punishment in Canada: A History.*
Toronto: McClelland and Stewart, 1991.

Chambers, Sheila, Joan Dawson and Edith Wolter. *Historic LaHave
River Valley.* Halifax: Nimbus Publishing, 2004.

Chiang, Hung-Min. *Chinese Islanders: Making a Home in the New
World.* Charlottetown: Island Studies Press, 2006.

Choyce, Lesley, ed. *Alternating Currents: Renewable Energy for
Atlantic Canada.* Halifax: Wooden Anchor Press, 1977.

Collins, Louis W. *In Halifax Town.* Halifax: Privately printed, 1975.

Cook, Francis. *Introduction to Canadian Amphibians and Reptiles.*
Ottawa: National Museum of Natural Sciences, 1984.

Cormier-Boudreau, Marielle and Melvin Gallant. *A Taste of Acadie.*
Fredericton: Goose Lane,1991.

Cornall, James. *Halifax South End.* Charleston: Arcadia Press, 1998.

Conrad, Margaret and James Hillier. *Atlantic Canada: A Region in
the Making.* Toronto: Oxford University Press, 2001.

Creighton, Helen. *Bluenose Magic.* Halifax: Nimbus Publishing,
2005.

Creighton, Helen. *Bluenose Magic: Popular Beliefs and Superstitions in
Nova Scotia.* Toronto: Ryerson, 1968.

Creighton, Helen. *Folklore of Lunenburg County, Nova Scotia.*
Toronto: McGraw-Hill Ryerson, 1976. Reprint of the National

Museum of Canada Bulletin Number 117, Anthropological Series Number 29, 1950.

Croft, Clary. *Chocolates, Tattoos and Mayflowers: Mainstreet Memorabilia from Clary Croft*. Halifax: Nimbus Publishing, 1995.

Croft, Clary. "Helen Creighton: Collecting the German-based Folklore of Lunenburg County, Nova Scotia," in *German-Canadian Yearbook*, Volume 16. Toronto: Historic Society of Mecklenburg Upper Canada, 2000.

Croft, Clary. *Nova Scotia Moments*. Halifax: Nimbus Publishing, 2004.

Davis, Stephen A. *The Micmac: People of the Maritimes*. Tantallon: Four East Publications, 1991.

DeCoste, John and Twila Robar-DeCoste. *The Little Wren Church: A History of St. Mary's Anglican Church*. Hantsport: Lancelot Press, 1990.

Denys, Nicholas. "Concerning the Ways of the Indians: their customs, dress, methods of hunting and fishing, and their amusements." First published in French, 1672. Nova Scotia Department of Education, n.d.

Drake, Caroline, ed. *A City's Journey: The Guardian*. Special 150th Anniversary edition, Charlottetown: 2005.

Dunlop, Allan C. "The Levee and other New Year's Festivities," in *Nova Scotia Historical Quarterly*. Vol. 10, No. 3-4. Royal Nova Scotia Historical Society,1980.

Duplacey, James. *Hockey's Book of Firsts*. North Dighton: JG Press, 2003.

Dwyer, Terry. *Wreck Hunter: The Quest for Lost Shipwrecks*. Lawrencetown Beach: Pottersfield Press, 2004.

Elliot, Shirley. *A History of Province House*. Province of Nova Scotia, n.d.

Erickson, Paul A. *Historic North End Halifax*. Halifax: Nimbus Publishing, 2004.

Explorer: Visitors Guide, Annapolis Royal, 2004.

Fauset, Arthur Huff. "Folklore from Nova Scotia," in *American Folklore Society*, Vol. 24. 1931.

Fergusson, C. Bruce. "Jewish Communities in Nova Scotia", in *Nova Scotia Journal of Education*, Vol. 11, No. 1, 1961.

Fergusson, C. Bruce. "The Floral Emblem of Nova Scotia," in *Nova Scotia Historical Quarterly*, Vol. 4, No. 1, March 1974.

Fergusson, Bruce and William Pope. *Glimpses into Nova Scotia*. Hantsport: Lancelot Press, 1974.

Fergusson, Donald A. *Beyond the Hebrides*. Halifax: Lawson Graphics Atlantic, 1977.

Fingard, Judith, Janet Guilford and David Sutherland. *Halifax: The First 250 Years*. Halifax: Formac, 1999.

Forsey, Eugene. "History of the Labour Movement in Canada," in *The Canadian Economy: Selected Readings*. Toronto: Macmillan, 1961.

Forsyth, Ian K. and Edith M. Rowlings. *A Goodly Heritage: Memories of North End Dartmouth, Early 1900s*. Dartmouth Heritage Association, 2002.

Friends of the Public Gardens. *The Halifax Public Gardens*. Halifax: Friends of the Public Gardens, 1989.

Fraser, Mary. *Folklore of Nova Scotia*. Antigonish: Formac Publishing, 1975. Reprint.

Furlong, Pauline. *Historic Amherst*. Halifax: Nimbus Publishing, 2001

Gesner, Claribel. *Cape Breton Anthology*. Windsor: Lancelot Press, 1972.

Gilhen, John. *Amphibians and Reptiles of Nova Scotia*. Halifax: Nova Scotia Museum, 1984.

Gillia, Rannie. *Historic North Sydney*. Halifax: Nimbus Publishing, 2005.

Goeb, Jan. *The Maritime Jewish Community*. Halifax: Halifax Jewish Historical Society, c.1975.

Graham, Monica. *Looking Back: Pictou County Nova Scotia*. St. Catherines: Looking Back Press, n.d.

Grant, B. J. *Fit to Print: New Brunswick Papers: 150 Years of the Comic, the Sad, the Odd, and the Forgotten*. Fredericton: Goose Lane, 1987.

Halifax and Its People 1749-1999: Images from Nova Scotia Archives and Record Management Halifax: Nimbus Publishing, 1999.

Halifax Daily News. "Nova Scotia: 100 Years in Review," in *Halifax Daily News* special supplement. Halifax: January 1, 2000.

Halifax Millennium Committee. *Wheels of Water, Wheels of Time.* Special advertising supplement by the *Halifax Herald.* Halifax: 2000.

Harvey, D. C. "Nova Scotia and the Canadian Naval Tradition," in *Canadian Historical Review,* Vol. 23. Toronto: University of Toronto Press, 1942.

Harvey, Robert Paton. *Historic Sackville.* Halifax: Nimbus Publishing, 2002.

Hector Enterprises. *Coming of the Hector 1773–1973.* Official Souvenir Program. New Glasgow: Hector Enterprises, 1973.

Heritage Trust of Nova Scotia. *Lakes, Salt Marshes and the Narrow Green Strip: Some Historic Buildings in Dartmouth and Halifax County's Eastern Shore.* 1979.

Saskatoon Women's Calendar Collective. *Her Story 2006: The Canadian Women's Calendar.* Regina: Coteau Books, 2006.

Jensen, L. B. *Nova Scotia Sketch Book.* Halifax: Petheric Press, c. 1969.

Jensen, L. B. *Vanishing Halifax.* Halifax: Petheric Press, 1968.

Julien, Donald. *Historical Perspective of Micmac Indians Pre & Post Contact Period.* Research paper prepared for the Confederacy of Mainland Micmac, c. 1988.

Kitz, Janet F. *Shattered City: The Halifax Explosion and the Road to Recovery.* Halifax: Nimbus Publishing, 1989.

Kitz, Janet. *Survivors: Children of the Halifax Explosion*. Halifax: Nimbus Publishing, 1992.

Knockwood, Noel. "Mythology and Religion of the Micmac People," in *Social Services News*. Halifax: Department of Social Services, 1975.

Labelle, Ronald. *Acadian Life in Chezzetcook*. Lawrencetown Beach: Pottersfield Press, 1995.

Leahey, Stephen. *Stories from the Lobster Fishery of Cumberland's Northern Shore*. Pugwash: North Cumberland Historical Society, 2005

MacBeath, George and Donald F. Taylor. *Steamboat Days on the St. John 1816 to 1946*. St. Stephen: Print'N Press, 1982

MacIntyre, John & Martha Walls. *Nova Scotia Book of Everything*. Lunenburg: MacIntyre Purcell Publishing, 2005.

Mackenzie, Shelagh, ed., with Scott Robson. *Halifax Street Names*. Halifax: Formac, 2002.

MacKenzie, Michael. *Tracks Across the Maritimes*. Christmas Island: MacKenzie Books, 1985.

Manny, Louise and James Reginald Wilson. *Songs of Miramichi*. Fredericton: Brunswick Press, 1976.

Marshall, Diane. *Georges Island: The Keeper of Halifax Harbour*. Halifax: Nimbus Publishing, 2003.

Marsters, Roger. *Shipwreck Treasures: Disaster and Discovery on Canada's East Coast*. Halifax: Formac Publishing, 2002.

Martell, James Stuart. *The Romance of Government House*. 3rd ed. Halifax: Department of Government Services, 1986.

Martin, John Patrick. *Halifax from the Citadel*. Halifax: City of Halifax, 1946.

M'Gregor, John. *British America*. Edinburgh: William Blackwood, 1832.

Metson, Graham. *An East Coast Port: Halifax at War 1939–1945*. Toronto: McGraw-Hill Ryerson, 1981.

"Mi'kmaq and First Nations Timeline (75,000 BC–2000 AD)," in *Shunpiking Magazine*, Fall 2005. Halifax: New Media Services Inc., 2005.

Milks, Robert E. *75 Years of Scouting in Canada*. Ottawa: Scouts Canada, 1982.

Morgan, Robert. *Early Cape Breton: From Founding to Famine*. Wreck Cove: Breton Books, 2000.

Morton, Desmond. *Wheels: The Car in Canada*. Toronto: Umbrella Press, 1998.

Nightingale, Marie. *Cooking with Friends*. Halifax: Nimbus Publishing, 2003.

Nightingale, Marie. *Out of Old Nova Scotian Kitchens*. Halifax: Petheric Press, 1970.

Nova Scotia Tourist Authority. *Halifax Nova Scotia: The Garrison City by the Sea*. Halifax: Nova Scotia Tourist Authority, c.1900.

Nowlan, Michael. *Ole Larsen's Miramichi: A Photographic Odyssey.* Halifax: Nimbus Publishing, 1999.

O'Neil, Pat. *A Traveller's Guide to Cape Breton.* Sydney: Solus Publishing, 1996.

O'Neill, Mora Dianne. *The Artist's Halifax: Portraits of the Town and Harbour through 250 Years.* Halifax: Formac Publishing, 2003.

Pachai, Bridglal and Henry Bishop. *Historic Black Nova Scotia.* Halifax: Nimbus Publishing, 2006.

Parker, Mike. *Historic Dartmouth: Reflections of Early Life.* Halifax: Nimbus Publishing, 1998.

Parker, Mike. *Woodchips & Beans: Life in the Early Lumber Woods of Nova Scotia.* Halifax: Nimbus Publishing, 1992.

Parks Canada. *Cradle of Confederation: Province House.* N.p.: Parks Canada, 1985.

Parks Canada. *Fort de Beauséjour/The Fort Beaséjour.* N.p.: Parks Canada, 1993.

Parks, M. G., ed. *Joseph Howe: Poems and Essays.* Toronto: University of Toronto Press, 1973.

Peck, Mary. *The Bitter with the Sweet: New Brunswick 1604–1984.* Tantallon: Four East Publications, 1983.

Perry, Hattie A. *Old Days Old Ways.* Tantallon: Four East Publications, 1989.

Pigott, Peter. *Gateways: Airports of Canada.* Lawrencetown Beach: Pottersfield Press, 1996.

Province of Nova Scotia. *A Map of the Province of Nova Scotia, 1992 Edition.* N.p.: Formac Publishing, 1992.

Quinpool, John. *First Things in Acadia.* Halifax: First Things Publishers Limited, 1936.

Raddall, Thomas Head. *Halifax: Warden of the North.* Garden City: Doubleday, 1965.

Rand, Silas T. *Legends of the Micmacs.* New York: Longmans, Green, and Company, 1894.

Rees, Ronald. *Historic St. Andrews.* Halifax: Nimbus Publishing, 2001.

Regan, John William. *Sketches of the Northwest Arm, Halifax, NS.* First published in 1908. Willowdale: Hounslow Press, 1978.

Regional Museums of Cultural History. *Paddles in Time: An exhibition of canoe and kayak sprint racing in Nova Scotia.* Dartmouth: 1997.

Roberts, Charles. *The Canadian Guide Book: The Tourist's and Sportsman's Guide to Eastern Canada and Newfoundland.* New York: D. Appleton, 1891.

Saucy, Leanne. *Backroad Mapbook, PEI. 2005.* Burnaby: Backroad Mapbook, 2005.

Seen, Roma. *The Haligonians: 100 Fascinating Lives from the Halifax Region.* Halifax: Formac Publishing, 2005.

Seto, William and Larry N. Shyu. *The Chinese Experience in New Brunswick: a historical perspective*. Fredericton: Chinese Cultural Association of New Brunswick, 1985.

Shyu, Larry N. *The Chinese: Peoples of the Maritimes*. Halifax: Nimbus Publishing, 1997.

Smith, Carrie-Ann. "Boomers from Abroad: The Children of Second World War Brides Celebrate Sixty Years in Canada," in *Boom Magazine*, Issue 5. Boutilier's Point: 2006.

Soucoup, Dan. *Historic New Brunswick*. Lawrencetown Beach: Pottersfield Press, 1997.

Soucoup, Dan. *Looking Back: from the Pages of the* Times and Transcript. Halifax: Maritime Lines, 2002.

Taylor, M. Brook. *A Camera on the Banks: Frederick William Wallace and the Fishermen of Nova Scotia*. Fredericton: Goose Lane, 2006.

Thurston, Harry. *Tidal Life: A Natural History of the Bay of Fundy*. Halifax: Nimbus Publishing, 1990.

Tourism, Culture, and Heritage, Halifax Regional Municipality and the Dartmouth Downtown Development Corporation. *Historic Dartmouth Walking Tour*. 2002.

Trotsky, Leon. *My Life*. New York: Charles Scribner's Sons, 1930.

Tufts, Robie W. *Birds of Nova Scotia*. 3rd ed. Halifax: Nimbus Publishing, 1986.

Bibliography

Vaughan, Garth. *Historic Windsor*. Halifax: Nimbus Publishing, 2006.

Watson, Julie V. *Ardgowan: A Journal of House and Garden in Victorian Prince Edward Island*. Charlottetown: Seacroft, 2000.

Watts, Heather and Michèle Raymond. *Halifax's Northwest Arm: An Illustrated History*. Halifax: Formac Publishing, 2003.

Whitehead, Ruth Holmes. *Elitekey: Micmac Material Culture from 1600 AD to the Present*. Halifax: NS Museum, 1980.

Whitehead, Ruth Holmes. *The Old Man Told Us: Excerpts from Micmac History 1500–1950*. Halifax: Nimbus Publishing, 1991.

Whitehead, Ruth Holmes and Harold McGee. *The Micmac: How Their Ancestors Lived Five Hundred Years Ago*. Halifax: Nimbus Publishing, 1983.

Wingfield-Stratford, Esmé. *Those Ernest Victorians*. New York: William Morrow, 1930.